HEARTWARMING STORIES OF ADVENTIST PIONEERS

Also by Norma J. Collins:
Heartwarming Stories of Adventist Pioneers:
You Will See Your Lord a-Coming
To order, **call 1-800-765-6955.**

Visit us at www.reviewandherald.com for information on other Review and Herald® products.

ON THE COVER:

1. Leonard Hastings
2. John N. Loughborough
3. Maude Sisley Boyd
4. Stephen N. Haskell

HEARTWARMING STORIES OF ADVENTIST PIONEERS

REVIEW AND HERALD® PUBLISHING ASSOCIATION
HAGERSTOWN, MD 21740

NORMA J. COLLINS

Copyright © 2007 by Review and Herald® Publishing Association

Published by Review and Herald® Publishing Association, Hagerstown, MD 21741-1119

All rights reserved. No portion of this book may be reproduced, stored in a retrieval system, or transmitted in any form or by any means (electronic, mechanical, photocopy, recording, scanning, or other), except for brief quotations in critical reviews or articles, without the prior written permission of the publisher.

Review and Herald® titles may be purchased in bulk for educational, business, fund-raising, or sales promotional use. For information, please e-mail SpecialMarkets@reviewandherald.com.

The Review and Herald® Publishing Association publishes biblically based materials for spiritual, physical, and mental growth and Christian discipleship.

The author assumes full responsibility for the accuracy of all facts and quotations as cited in this book.

Because of this book's informality, quotations throughout it, though accurate, are not always reproduced verbatim.

This book was
Edited by Penny Estes Wheeler
Copyedited by James Cavil
Cover design and photo illustration by Trent Truman
Cover photos from Review and Herald Collection
Electronic makeup by Shirley M. Bolivar
Typeset: Bembo 11/14

PRINTED IN U.S.A.

11 10 09 08 07   5 4 3 2 1

Review and Herald Cataloging Services
Collins, Norma J.
    Heartwarming stories of Adventist pioneers.

    1. Seventh-day Adventists—History. 2. Seventh-day Adventists—Biography.
3. Seventh-day Adventist Church—History.   I. Title.

286.732

ISBN 978-0-8280-2014-5

In Memory of

Elder Arthur L. White,

my friend and mentor, who
first introduced me to the
Adventist pioneers.
1907-1991

With Thanks to:

James R. Nix, who encouraged and cheered me on through the writing of this book; Kenneth H. Wood, for his careful teaching and example through the years; Jocelyn Fay, for her friendship and encouragement; Jeannette Johnson, for starting me on the road to the two volumes of *Heartwarming Stories of the Pioneers;* Penny Estes Wheeler, for her patience and skill through the long editing process; the Review and Herald Publishing Association personnel, especially in the manufacturing and book divisions.

Contents

A Word to the Reader 9

CHAPTER

1   Leonard Hastings: The Potato Patch Preacher 11

2   Maude Sisley Boyd: A Woman of Firsts 16

3   Ellen G. White: Part 1, She Labored On Alone 19

4   Ellen G. White: Part 2, The Salamanca Vision 32

5   Ellen G. White: Part 3, Australia Beckons 38

6   Ellen G. White: Part 4, Needed Back in America 49

7   Frederick Wheeler: First Ordained Minister to Preach the Sabbath 60

8   Anna Knight: Missionary to India and the South 65

9   Nathaniel D. Faulkhead: Secret Societies 84

10   Stephen Nelson Haskell: "Man of Action" 88

11   Hetty Hurd: The Woman God Wanted 104

12   Stephen and Hetty Hurd Haskell: Joining Their Lives in God's Work 107

13   Marian Davis: Book Maker Extraordinary 118

14   Alma Baker McKibbin: Author of the "Shoestring Books" .127

15   Stephen Smith: The Unwanted Testimony in the Trunk . . .146

16   John Norton Loughborough: Part 1, "Fear God and Give Glory to Him" 152

17   John Norton Loughborough: Part 2, California Ho! 174

    Bibliography 187

A Word to the Reader

Book Two of *Heartwarming Stories of the Adventist Pioneers* is a continuation of Book One, with others of the pioneers taking center stage. The result is a two-volume series giving a fresh new look at these self-sacrificing pioneers who spent their lives, their health, their pennies—and their fortunes—in spreading the three angels' messages.

The subtitle of Book Two was chosen because of the book's strong emphasis on the fact that these pioneers also earnestly labored for souls for the kingdom of God. They've left a lasting legacy in the fact that "their works do follow them." Men and women were, and are, led to Christ through remembering the sacrifices of those early pioneers. The title of Book Two is taken directly from their legacy: *Their Works Do Follow Them*.

To open his evangelistic meetings James White frequently used a song he had come to love, "You Will See Your Lord a-Coming." Some of the most often repeated stories of those early days begin with the account of Elder White walking down an aisle in a meeting place or schoolhouse singing:

> "You will see your Lord a-coming,
> You will see your Lord a-coming,
> You will see your Lord a-coming,
>   In a few more days.
>   Hear the band of music,
>   Hear the band of music,
>   Hear the band of music
>   Which is sounding thro' the air."

The sentiments of this song, and sometimes the words, are carried over in Book Two.

The word "adventist" was used in the early days to designate one who believed in or preached the soon coming of Jesus. This was long before the organization of the Seventh-day Adventist Church and is understood as a generic term to identify those who believed that the second advent of Jesus was very near.

In Book Two you'll meet Anna Knight, who as a young girl fell in love with Jesus. At the same time, she learned about the Sabbath and wanted more than anything to be baptized into the Seventh-day Adventist Church. To accomplish this simple act, she had to travel 382 miles. As the only Adventist in her family she often spent the entire Sabbath by herself, memorizing the Sabbath school lesson or reading the Christian magazines that came her way.

Then you'll get new insights into the life of N. D. Faulkhead of Australia, a man intimately associated with the Masons and other secret societies.

Elder S. N. Haskell makes his appearance in this volume, along with Hetty Hurd Haskell, his second wife. They worked together spreading the gospel message for more than 20 years. You'll hold your breath as you read of their exciting assignment in dealing with the holy flesh movement at the Indiana camp meeting of 1900.

And you'll feel Mrs. White's pain as she struggles to keep her promise to her husband to carry forward the work of spreading the gospel message. And carry it forward she did—not only in the United States but also in Europe and Australia. Marian Davis, Ellen White's "book maker," gives insights into how Mrs. White's work was done and what happened one memorable day when a window was left open.

Through these stories and others you'll learn of the hardships, the sorrows, and the joys as our heroes lived their lives in harmony with God's will. They gladly followed His leading, doing their best to spread the news of Jesus' soon coming to take His children to the heavenly home He's preparing for them.

As you review the lives of these consecrated men and women of God, my fondest hope is that you will be led to rededicate your own life to the service of Jesus—your best friend—who died that you might live forever with Him.

My prayer for all of us is that we too will be so committed to following our Lord that we'll be willing to do whatever He asks us to, and to go wherever He sends us. I pray that each of us will stand firm until Jesus comes in the clouds of glory to take us home with Him.

Norma J. Collins

~ Chapter 1 ~

Leonard Hastings: The Potato Patch Preacher

Great excitement swept through the ranks as the Millerites did their best to tell as many as possible the good news that Jesus was coming very soon. But believing them to be ignorant and deceived, most people paid little attention. Nevertheless, the Millerites tried to show by their lives that they truly believed that Jesus was returning to earth on October 22, 1844, to take the saved to heaven.

One of those who faithfully gave the good news and warning was Leonard Hastings, a farmer in New Hampshire. His primary business was pasturing and caring for cattle that were driven up from Massachusetts for the summer. But he grew enough produce to supply his family's needs and a potato crop that he sold for some income. The Hastings family lived near the town of New Ipswich, the center of a Millerite Adventist community that spread out in a radius of about 10 miles. Leonard Hastings, the local leader of the group, and was firm in his belief of Jesus' soon return.

In the spring of 1844 Hastings had put in a large field of potatoes. They grew well, and were ready for harvest in the fall. But Hastings felt it would be a denial of his faith to dig them. After all, Jesus was coming in a few more weeks, and he would have no need of them. When word got around that he wasn't digging his potatoes, a few of his neighbors offered to dig them for him and put them in his barn. But Hastings was sure he wouldn't need the potatoes, and by not digging them he would proclaim his faith that Jesus would indeed come on October 22.

"No," he said, "I'm going to let that field of potatoes preach my faith in the Lord's soon coming."

"He's foolish," the neighbors told each other.

"He'll be sorry," others declared behind his back. "The potatoes will rot in the ground."

But Leonard Hastings wasn't swayed by their unbelief. Along with other Millerites he demonstrated by his actions what he had discovered from Bible study. He looked for Christ's immediate return. He longed for it. And all through the day and night of October 22 Hastings and the other believers watched and waited. When, at last, the clocks tolled midnight and Jesus hadn't come, they were devastated. October 22, 1844, became known as the Great Disappointment.

But what happened to the Millerite believers after the Disappointment and while they continued to search the Scriptures to understand the reason Christ did not come that day? Did those who hadn't harvested their crops face starvation? What happened to Mr. Hastings' potato patch? Did his potatoes indeed rot in the ground?

No. None of the Millerites starved to death—not even Leonard Hastings. He had said he wanted his potatoes to preach his faith in Jesus. As it turned out, his potatoes did a better job of preaching than he himself could have done.

The fall of 1844 was mild, and Hastings' potatoes were left in the ground until November. When he finally dug them, he found that they were some of the best he'd ever grown. However, his neighbors, who had dug their potatoes on schedule, didn't fare so well. A potato blight came to New England that year, rotting nearly all the potatoes that had been dug at the proper time. But the ones left in the ground didn't rot! So Mr. Hastings had a big supply of potatoes for his family—as well as for those same neighbors who had called him foolish.

A bonus came the next spring when it was time to plant potatoes again. Many of Hastings' neighbors and acquaintances came to him to buy seed potatoes to plant in their gardens and fields. Because of the scarce supply, seed potatoes sold for as much as $5 a bushel—an enormous price. What the people thought was going to cause Leonard Hastings a lot of trouble turned out to be a great blessing to him—and also to his neighbors!

By 1847 Hastings and his wife had not yet met James and Ellen White in person, although they had exchanged some correspondence. Apparently the first letter was written by James White to Elvira Hastings, for he says, "All I know of you is from what I have seen in the *Day-Dawn* from your pen. . . . When I get anything good I have a desire that all the faithful should share a slice. This is my apology for addressing you at this time and enclosing these two visions to you."

James had just received copies of the broadside that Joseph Bates had helped him publish. It carried Ellen White's vision confirming the Sabbath truth. Along with this he sent a copy of the 1846 broadside containing Ellen's first visions.

When in 1849 James and Ellen White were able to make a visit to the Hastings family, they found them in "deep affliction." Elvira Hastings met them with tears, saying "The Lord has sent you to us in a time of great need!" The problem was that Leonard and Elvira's 8-week-old baby cried continually. Nothing could comfort the child nor ease the pain that was causing the distress. Elvira herself was in a bad state of health, and had about reached the end of her rope.

Sizing up the situation, James and Ellen White suggested that they pray for the healing of both mother and child. They knelt and followed the instruction in James 5:14, 15 to pray for the sick. Using a little oil, they anointed the baby, and as they prayed the infant became quiet and soon fell asleep. Both Elvira and her child were healed, and peace and efficiency once again reigned in the household.

Both Mr. and Mrs. Hastings were more grateful than they could express. Ellen White, too, felt that their time with this family was very precious. She and Elvira seemed to be kindred spirits, for she wrote that "the heart of Sister Hastings [was] knit with mine as were those of David and Jonathan. Our union was not marred while she lived."

About a year later, in 1850, the Whites received news of Elvira Hastings' sudden death. She was only 42 years old. Apparently she died of a ruptured appendix.

Ellen White wrote to Leonard Hastings, "The news of your wife's death was to me overwhelming. I could hardly believe it and can hardly believe it now. God gave me a view last Sabbath night which I will write. . . . I saw that she was sealed and would come up at the voice of God and stand upon the earth, and would be with the 144,000. I saw we need not mourn for her; she would rest in the time of trouble, and all that we could mourn for was our loss in being deprived of her company. I saw her death would result in good."

What a comforting message this must have been to Leonard Hastings and his four children. Ellen White remembered the Hastings children, often writing cheerful little motherly notes to them, encouraging them to give their hearts and lives to Jesus.

Leonard Hastings served on nominating and auditing committees when the New England Conference was organized in 1870, and he was vice president of the New England Tract and Missionary Society, New Ipswich, New Hampshire. He died in 1882.

Vignettes

Leonard Hastings' potato crop wasn't the only potato crop that preached a sermon.

Silas Guilford, William Miller's brother-in-law, had moved from Dresden, New York, to near Oswego, New York, and had planted a 12-acre field of potatoes in the spring of 1844. When October 22, 1844, was set as the date Jesus would come, Silas, along with others, left his potatoes in the ground as a testimony of his faith in the Lord's coming. The snows came early around Oswego that year and covered the acres of potatoes. They stayed in the ground all winter.

When spring came and the snow melted, Silas mentioned to his wife that he was "going up to the potato field and see if any of the potatoes survived the winter."

"Oh, Silas," she pleaded, "we've been the joke of the town. If people see you up there digging around in the ground, they'll start all over again. Just let it go; besides, you know all of the potatoes froze through the winter, and now they're rotten."

"Well, Irving and I'll just go and take a look," he told her. (Irving, his son, was the young man who had ridden his horse 16 miles from Dresden, New York, to his uncle William Miller's house to invite him to come and tell their neighbors about Jesus.)

Irving reported that his father put his turning fork into the thawed ground and found, in the very first hill, nice, firm potatoes. They had not been frozen at all, and there was no rot in any of them. The next hill was the same. And the next!

In great excitement Silas Guliford sent Irving back to the house to get the other boys. They came running, carrying their turning forks and spades. They dug up the whole 12 acres, which yielded an awesome number of wonderful potatoes. They got $4.50 a bushel for them. The sale of the potatoes made enough money for Silas Guilford to pay off his mortgage and have a good nest egg left over. Surely God honored the faith of His followers.

Chapter 2

Maude Sisley Boyd: A Woman of Firsts

The strangers came timidly into the tent meeting in Battle Creek on the Sabbath after the organization of the General Conference in May 1863. Ellen White recognized them as a family she had seen in vision. She also had seen some of them as future workers in the cause of God. She leaned over and whispered excitedly to her husband, "James, do you see that woman coming in with the children? They've come over from England so they can keep the Sabbath."

Just a few weeks earlier Mrs. White had seen this family in vision—while they were still at home in England. She saw them as they studied the Bible and sought help from various ministers and Bible workers as they searched to understand the meaning of the fourth commandment.

A short break in the program gave her the opportunity to ask the whole family to come up to the platform. She was eager to have all those in the audience welcome these newcomers to America.

Ellen White mentioned several incidents in the life of this English family. She knew about the father's death; she had been shown that it was caused by the doctor giving medicines that were "too powerful." At the conclusion of her little speech she remarked that all of these children would one day be workers in the cause of God.

Maude, one of the Sisley girls, was 16 when she went to work in the typesetting department at the Review and Herald Publishing Association. She reported that Elder and Mrs. White always reminded the workers that as they went about the mechanical work of preparing the literature for distribution, they were preaching the third angel's message as surely as was the minister in the pulpit. Maude and her coworkers learned to appreciate the privilege of working in the cause of God in whatever way opened before them.

A woman of firsts, in September 1868 Maude Sisley attended the first official Seventh-day Adventist camp meeting at Wright, Michigan. When the tithing plan began to be accepted by the church members in Battle Creek, she was one of the first to pay tithe. She also became a charter member of Battle Creek's first Tract Society, an organization that had its beginnings in South Lancaster, Massachusetts, under the direction of S. N. Haskell.

So enthusiastic was she about sharing her faith that Maude decided to join another young woman, Elsie Gates, as a partner in literature work. Making their headquarters in Newark, Ohio, they rented an attic room for 50 cents a month. They spent many happy months working in Newark, where they lived on about 25 cents a week.

Maude had been a member of the church for about 10 years and had often thought she was willing to do anything her Lord wanted her to do. And she thought she meant it. Then one early evening while kneeling in prayer, she distinctly heard a voice ask her, "Are you willing to do *anything* the Lord wants you to do?"

With this question came a very deep impression that the Lord was going to ask her to do something she wouldn't want to do.

Kneeling there, she came face to face with the realization that she had not made that wholehearted surrender she thought she had. She couldn't seem to say the words, "Yes, Lord, I'll do whatever You ask."

She knew in her heart that she was standing before the Judge of the universe. Unless she could say with certainty that His will was hers, her fate was sealed. She prayed and wept, but there was no relief from her certainty of condemnation. Finally, about midnight she confessed, "Oh, Lord Jesus, I do love You, I do. But I can't make the complete surrender of my life in my own strength. But Jesus, I'm *willing for You to do the work for me."*

Immediately a great peace of mind and heart flooded her soul. She held her own little praise service there in the wee hours of the morning, then slept soundly until the dawn of the new day.

The *very next morning* she received a letter from the General Conference inviting her to go to Switzerland to assist Elder J. N. Andrews in the publishing work in Basel. She was certain she would not have accepted the invitation had the angel of the Lord not visited her the evening before.

Accordingly, in 1877 Maude Sisley became the first Seventh-day Adventist single woman called to serve in a foreign mission field. Working with J. N. Andrews, in true pioneer spirit she learned to set type in a language she didn't know—producing the first Seventh-day Adventist tract in Italian. Two years later she was called to Southampton, England. Her help was needed as a Bible instructor there, and J. N. Loughborough became her mentor.

A year or two later she returned to the United States, where she married C. L. Boyd, a widower and president of the Nebraska Conference. They later did pioneer work in the Northwest, where he was president of the North Pacific Conference.

Maude and her husband were a part of the first group of missionaries sent to Africa in 1887. Because of health problems they had to return to the United States in 1891, leaving part of their hearts in a tiny grave where their little Ethel rests till Jesus comes. Elder Boyd died in 1898 and is buried in North Carolina.

After her husband's death, Maude visited her sister Nellie (Mrs. G. B. Starr) in Australia. Her mother, then 79 years old and known as Grandma Sisley, went with her. Maude taught at Avondale College, and later served as a Bible instructor in New South Wales and Victoria. After returning to America, she served for another 17 years as a Bible instructor at the Loma Linda and Glendale sanitariums in California.

In 1922 Mrs. Boyd wrote to the retirement office of the General Conference and explained to them that she was not in real need of the financial help they had been giving her. They responded by agreeing to stop her payments, but assured her that if she should need it at any time, they would be happy to reinstate it.

When she was 76, her position at Loma Linda Sanitarium was needed by a younger person, and she willingly resigned. Now she was ready for retirement, and asked that her monthly allowance be resumed. But she didn't retire to her rocking chair on the front porch. For several more years she spent four to five hours a day visiting and studying the Bible with patients at the sanitarium.

Maude Sisley Boyd died in 1937 at the age of 86. Surely her works do follow her.

Chapter 3

Ellen G. White:

Part 1
She Labored On Alone

As Ellen stood beside her husband's deathbed in 1881, she tenderly took his hand in hers and spoke to him: "James, my dear, dear husband, through the years you've always taken care of all the business matters and developed and led out in new ventures for the Lord. Now I promise you to be a pioneer myself. If you understand my words, squeeze my hand just a little." Although he couldn't speak, James White tightened his hand in hers. A short time later he closed his eyes in death.

Through God's guidance and with His sustaining grace, Ellen White fulfilled her promise to James. As the work began in Europe, she spent two years there, giving her testimony for God and teaching and encouraging the believers. She pioneered the work in Australia, spending nearly 10 years there. Both overseas and in the United States she constantly was in demand for speaking appointments at various camp meetings and committee meetings, and for counsel about different phases of the rapidly expanding work of God. Through instruction from God she was instrumental in locating properties for schools, sanitariums, hospitals, and churches.

While she was doing all this, she also was writing—letters of personal counsel, articles, and books, trying to fulfill her promise to James that she would be a pioneer herself.

But let's go back to Battle Creek and the days following the death of James White.

A small group of men came to speak to Ellen about a monument for her husband's grave. They wanted to put up a broken shaft, signifying that his work was cut short and that no one else could carry on in his place. Her reaction was swift and firm: "Never! Never! He has done single-handedly the work of three men. *Never* shall a broken monument be placed over his grave!"

She suggested that they put up a full, perfect monument. He had completed his work. She knew that at the trump of God he would "see his Lord a-coming."

White's Ranch in Colorado

Having buried her beloved husband in beautiful Oak Hill Cemetery, Ellen was sorely in need of rest. She felt that their home in the mountains of Colorado would be the best place to get her bearings now that she was a widow. Her daughters-in-law, Mary and Emma, accompanied her. The three of them spent a few days in Boulder with Emma's parents, the McDearmons; then Ellen and Mary headed for "White's Ranch," near Rollinsville.

Mary Clough, Ellen's niece, had homesteaded the acreage, complete with a small cabin, securing the title in 1873. James White bought it from Mary in 1876. Over the years he added another 160 acres and enlarged the cabin. This was "White's Ranch," where Ellen hoped to find rest and comfort. But it wasn't the same without James. True, she slept better there, and her health did seem to improve, but she wasn't able to do any writing.

Everywhere she looked she remembered the happy, restful times she and James had spent there together. Now she felt so very alone. Although she knew that God's ways were always best, the beautiful Colorado mountains had lost their charm for her.

She was torn between returning to her new home in Battle Creek, where she would be comfortable for the winter, and going on to California to rest and to try to recoup her strength and energy. California finally won over the stress of responsibilities that would be hers in Battle Creek.

California

On October 2, 1881, Mrs. White boarded one of the chugging, smoke-belching little trains that she and James had so often traveled on together, leaving Colorado and its memories behind. She arrived in Sacramento in time to attend the opening service of the camp meeting on October 13. In spite of her weakened physical condition, she spoke at the meetings almost every afternoon.

Still not ready to take up a strenuous writing program, she spent most of her time during the rest of 1881 and early 1882 visiting various churches in California. Much of the travel to those churches was by carriage—with Ellen White as the driver and a Brother Harmon leading the way in his wagon. She described a 35-mile trip from Healdsburg to St. Helena:

"The road through Knight's Canyon, always perilous to the inexperienced traveler, is often impassable in the rainy season. . . . I dared not look either to the right or left to view the scenery, but, holding the lines firmly, and guiding my horse in the narrow passage, I followed our leader. Carelessness here would have been fatal. Had our horse turned out of the right path, we should have plunged down a steep precipice, into the ravine below."

After visiting the various churches for several months, Ellen decided to make Healdsburg her home. She and James had a little farm on West Dry Creek Road, about three miles from Healdsburg. There she had all the conveniences she needed. She could keep a cow and chickens, and fruits and vegetables were cheap. Best of all, she could be happy there, and it was where she wanted to be. To her this was a temporary arrangement. She was testing the waters to see what her health could withstand. If it became necessary, she could go to the St. Helena Sanitarium. In the meantime, she would live at the Healdsburg "White's Ranch."

The next year she moved a little closer to town, buying a two-story house on Powell Street. Her newly acquired orchards produced an abundant harvest of plums and peaches, which she canned for her own use and for those in need. She declared this chore to be rest for her weary brain. God provided an extra blessing in the income she received from renting her spare rooms to some of the construction workers at the new college.

Miraculous Healing

While on a speaking trip to Oakland in August, Ellen became very ill. After several weeks she was taken to St. Helena Sanitarium, but she didn't seem to improve. She pleaded with her son Willie to take her home to Healdsburg, where the California camp meeting was scheduled to open in October. She hoped she would be strong enough to give her testimony.

The first Sabbath of camp meeting arrived, and she still was hardly able to leave her bed. Nonetheless, she asked Willie to make arrangements for her in the big tent, placing her special chair where she could hear the speaker. Perhaps just being there and being able to hear the speaker would revive her. She sat in her chair, weak and deathly pale.

J. H. Waggoner, editor of *Signs of the Times,* was the main speaker, and when he finished his message, Mrs. White asked Willie to assist her to the pulpit. She wanted to say a few words to the people. She later wrote that she thought this would be her farewell message. Placing both hands on the pulpit, she stood there for several minutes, trying to speak. "All at once I felt a power come upon me, like a shock of electricity. It passed through my body and up to my head. The people said that they plainly saw the blood mounting to my lips, my ears, my cheeks, my forehead."

All eyes were upon her. One of the community leaders, Mr. Montrose, stood up and exclaimed, "We are seeing a miracle performed before our eyes; Mrs. White is healed!"

Her voice grew stronger, and she gave a testimony such as they had never heard before. She made an altar call for those who wanted to serve God, and urged those who had wandered away from God to recommit their lives to their heavenly Father. More than a few in the large audience responded to the call.

Because she had been seriously ill for two months, it was as if she had been raised from the dead. This miraculous, very public healing marked a decided upturn in her physical condition. She was able to resume her work for the Lord with renewed energy and dedication. She declared, "It cannot be attributed to imagination. The people saw me in my feebleness, and many remarked that to all appearances I was a candidate for the grave. Nearly all present marked the changes which took place in me while I was addressing them. . . . I testify to all who read these words, that the Lord has healed me."

Back to Work

Her writing and speaking resumed. After attending the Eastern camp meetings, Ellen arrived in Battle Creek in time for the Michigan camp meeting and the General Conference session. At that meeting an action was taken recommending republication of the *Testimonies* in four volumes. Her writing on the life of Christ, as it appeared in *Spirit of Prophecy,* volumes 2 and 3, was to be published in a single volume. Marian Davis, a young woman who had joined her as a literary assistant in 1879, was assigned to see the project through to publication.

Finishing her work in Battle Creek, Mrs. White returned home just in time to spend New Year's Eve (1884) in Healdsburg, where she was happy to participate in the celebration of a Sabbath school reunion. She was pleased that an appropriate program was provided to make the holidays a happy and memorable time for the young people and children.

The Great Controversy Goes to Press

At long last, in the fall of 1884, *Spirit of Prophecy,* volume 4, *The Great Controversy Between Christ and Satan,* was ready. Both the Pacific Press and the Review and Herald published 5,000 copies simultaneously. The first edition was completely sold out on the West Coast by the end of the year.

With *The Great Controversy* in print, Mrs. White felt free to accept some of the urgent camp meeting appointments that had come to her. At the meeting in Maine she had a few hours to visit her twin sister, Elizabeth, who was crippled with rheumatism. They very much enjoyed their visit together, but Ellen was sorry to have to leave her sister in such an incapacitated and painful condition.

The Michigan Camp Meeting

The Michigan camp meeting in 1884 was much larger than expected. The 80' x 120' main tent was surrounded by a city of tents. Almost 200 cotton tents and pavilions were laid out in street formation, so any family could easily be located. Approximately 1,800 people camped in the tents or roomed in private homes nearby. A special train brought 240 college students and workers from the sanitarium in Battle Creek. On several occasions 200 to 350 people responded to Ellen White's appeals and went forward for prayers.

Dudley Canright

The Spirit of the Lord was abundantly present at the 1884 Michigan camp meeting, and Elder Dudley Canright repented (again) of his backslidden condition. He confessed and repented of his bitter feelings toward Ellen White because of the unvarnished testimonies she had been obliged to send him. Unfortunately, a few years later he made his final departure from the Adventist Church.

The news came as no surprise to Mrs. White. A short time earlier she had been given a dream in which she was shown Canright on a well-worn but sturdy ship sailing through rough waters. Seeing a better-looking vessel nearby, he decided it was more trustworthy and would take him safely to his destination. He was warned that its timbers were rotten and riddled with worms; that if he made the transfer, he was headed for destruction. In spite of the repeated cautions, he jumped ship and went over to the more attractive vessel.

In a matter of months Canright was preaching for another denomination. Contrary to his departing promises that his best friends were among the Adventists and that he would never oppose them, he soon became a bitter enemy of the Seventh-day Adventist Church. He did everything in his power to discredit both the church and Ellen White.

Missionary to Europe

At the 1884 General Conference session a request was presented from the committee of the Central European Mission that Ellen White spend some time in Europe so that new believers could benefit from her personal experience as the messenger of the Lord.

At first Mrs. White couldn't see her way clear to go to Europe. Not only was she getting older, but she had her health to consider. As she prayed about the matter, she couldn't seem to get a direct yes or no answer.

The time came when a final decision had to be made. Willie went from Oakland to Healdsburg to spend a few days with his mother. In trying to help her make a decision, he suggested that she look at past times when she had moved by faith under some very discouraging conditions but had depended upon the best light she had at the moment.

As she did so, she felt she should trust the judgment of the General Conference brethren. Her trunk was already packed—just in case—and she returned to Oakland with Willie. There she was asked to speak to the church members on Sabbath afternoon. As she hesitated, the words of Jesus came to her: *My grace is sufficient for you.*

Those words sustained her and her fears vanished, yet her weakness remained. But when she stood to speak, she felt God's everlasting arms beneath her, and she was given physical strength and mental clearness to speak with power the words He gave her. From that time onward her courage increased, and she was sure of the journey ahead.

The invitation to spend time in Europe also included Ellen White's son W. C. White; his wife, Mary; and their small daughter, Ella. Sara McEnterfer was chosen to be Mrs. White's traveling companion and attendant. As the travelers found their seats on the train headed east, Ellen was filled with certainty that she was in harmony with God's will. His peace enveloped her, and she found rest in Jesus. She was 57, and this was her twenty-fifth trip from one U.S. coast to the other.

Their ship, the S.S. *Cephalonia,* was to leave Boston harbor on Sabbath afternoon, so they boarded on Friday afternoon in order to be settled and ready when the Sabbath arrived. At sundown the whole group gathered in Ellen's stateroom for worship. A week later they landed in Liverpool.

After a miserable trip across the rough waters of the English Channel, they traveled by train to Basel, Switzerland, where they were met by Elder B. L. Whitney, president of the Swiss Mission. They were taken immediately to the publishing house, where they met many of the workers. The pressroom was on the ground floor, and as Mrs. White entered the room she saw that the press was running. She remarked that she had "seen this press before," and that the room looked very familiar to her.

Two young men were introduced to her. Shaking hands with them, she asked, "Where is the other one?"

"What other one?" asked Whitney.

"There's an older man here, and I have a message for him."

It was explained that the foreman of the pressroom had gone into the city on business. Ten years earlier, in Battle Creek, Ellen White was shown the work being done in this very pressroom, along with the foreman who supervised the workers there. This little snippet of information brought renewed courage to all those associated with the work in Basel.

Mrs. White's Work in Europe Begins

Mrs. White was given an apartment in the publishing house building, and from this "headquarters" she branched out to neighboring cities, villages, and other countries over the next two years. Soon after her arrival she met with the European Council of Seventh-day Adventist Missions. A Bible institute, as well as public evangelism, was planned, and problems unique to Europe were discussed.

On one occasion a group met to give consideration to new plans for advancing the work in several countries. Daniel Bourdeau proposed that France and Italy not join with the Swiss Mission but become a separate conference, using their own money to build up their conference. Ellen White could see that this would lead to disagreement and friction in the work. It would separate their interests and weaken the work as a whole.

As she spoke in general terms, mentioning no names, Daniel Bourdeau jumped up and hotly took her remarks as being directed toward him personally. He didn't attend the meeting the rest of the day and packed his things to leave.

Feeling that she must speak with Daniel again, but hardly daring to think that she could because of his "defiant, stubborn spirit," Mrs. White paced the floor in distress. She knew she must make the effort, for it seemed to her that Bourdeau was in a life-and-death struggle with evil powers. She prayed for guidance and then sent not only for Daniel and his wife to come to her room, but also his brother, A. C. Bourdeau, as well as B. L. Whitney, S. H. Lane, and W. C. White.

She began to speak directly to Daniel, but he interrupted her. She had hurt his feelings, he said, and he felt the other men had turned against him; he would rather see her alone. In no uncertain terms she asked him to be quiet because she had a message from God for him. He subsided somewhat, and then she spoke, giving him "such a message as I wish never to speak again to mortal man."

She strongly urged him not to leave the building until the power of Satan was broken in his mind and heart. Then they all knelt and prayed. She said that Daniel "prayed for himself rather faintly." A terrible struggle was going on in Daniel Bourdeau, but he couldn't seem to make a full surrender to God. He looked as though his soul and his body were "rent asunder." The Sabbath was only hours away.

Ellen was afraid that Daniel wouldn't come that evening to the meeting that had been planned especially for the ministers and their wives. Bourdeau wasn't the only one whose pet project had been shot down, but he seemed to be the only one who was so vocally hostile. For example, A. A. John, from England, didn't get any encouragement for his plan to hold large meetings—with large expenses—at the places where the wealthy gathered during the vacation season. It was an expensive project that had little hope of any real success. And there were others.

But to Ellen's surprise, Daniel came to the meeting. Her diary tells the story:

"The Spirit of the Lord rested upon me, and I prayed for light and grace from heaven. . . . His Spirit came into our meeting in large measure. Hearts were broken before Him.

"Brother Daniel Bourdeau wrenched himself from the shackles of Satan, and surrendered his will to the Lord. Satan had thought to gain the victory over this brother, but he was signally defeated. Angels of God were in the meeting, and the power of God was felt."

At the meeting on Sabbath afternoon, she bore testimony of encouragement to others who were present, one of whom was Martha Bourdeau, wife of A. C. Bourdeau:

"Jesus loves you. Why gather about your soul the clouds of darkness? Why walk in a fog of unbelief? Come just as you are, helpless and hopeless.

"My sister, have you not every encouragement to gather up your confidence? Have you endeavored not only to believe in Christ but to live in your daily life as His disciple?"

Martha is the sad, discouraged woman Ellen White describes in pages 116 and 117 of *Steps to Christ*. She walks through a beautiful garden in sadness. Wandering from the path, she finds herself in a tangle of briars and thorns. She sees only that the garden is spoiled by thorns; she doesn't see the roses, the lilies, and the pinks that she could be gathering for her own and others' happiness.

By Sunday morning there were many encouraging responses to Mrs. White's testimony, including Martha Bourdeau's. She pledged that henceforth she would trust in God. She vowed that she would no longer walk in darkness. She would cast out her doubts and speak only of the love of Jesus, her Savior.

Ministering in Scandinavia

The White party left for Scandinavia on October 6. It was not a good time to go north, for it was already very cold there. But because she had seen the condition of some of these churches in vision many years before, Mrs. White felt that she should go as soon as possible.

Both Willie and Mary were part of the group, though their little daughter remained in Basel with Sara McEnterfer, Mrs. White's traveling companion. Meetings were held in Copenhagen, where Ellen White spoke five times. Then it was on to Sweden. There they spent several days in Stockholm, visiting the members and holding meetings.

In Christiania (now Oslo), Norway, they stayed in the home of A. B. Oyen, a minister sent over from Battle Creek to translate the Ellen White books. They spent two weeks in Norway holding meetings. Most of the meetings were in Christiania, where a new publishing house was being built, and there Ellen spoke in the Good Templars' Hall, as well as in other public halls. At Drammen, a city about 30 miles from Christiania, the members rented the largest hall they could find, which seated about 700.

There was no speakers' platform, so men brought six beer tables from another room to make a platform. Another table was set on top of those tables to serve as a pulpit, and steps to the platform were created with chairs and stools. Mrs. White opined, "We doubt if the hall or beer tables were ever put to so good use before. The people came and filled the seats, the galleries, and all the standing room, and listened with the best of attention while I spoke to them of the love of Christ, and His life of sacrifice."

As their trip to Scandinavia was coming to a close, W. C. White was convinced that he should attend the 1885 General Conference session, which would begin on November 18 in Battle Creek. He finally brought up the subject with his mother, and as they talked about it she also was convicted that this was something he should do. He could give a full report to the session on the work in Europe and how the needs could be met. Two days later he took the ferry across the North Sea to England. From Liverpool he would sail to New York, and from there travel by train to Battle Creek. He would return in two months.

The Last Meeting in Christiania

Willie had left on Friday, and on Sabbath morning Ellen White met with the congregation in Christiania. During the week she had written a 16-page testimony to this church, and Elder A. B. Oyen had already translated much of it into Norwegian. On Sabbath afternoon he read that portion of it to the church. The next afternoon, Sunday, she met with the church in a final service at the Good Templars' Hall.

She thought she would be able to slip away from the hall unnoticed during the singing of the closing hymn. But when she reached her carriage, she found that many of the people were waiting for her. With tears and expressions of gratitude and love they said their goodbyes, urging her to come again. Afterward she felt sorry that she hadn't remained in the hall to shake hands with every last one of them. Before dawn the next morning she was at the train station, as were a large number of the believers waiting to give her a loving send-off.

The return trip to Basel took four days. They had been gone six weeks, traveling more than 2,500 miles. But there was no time for a good rest, for she would be leaving less than a week later on a trip to Italy.

Italy

On Mrs. White's fifty-eighth birthday, November 26, she was on the train headed for Torre Pellice. She had been in Europe but a short time, and already she had been hard at work in England, Switzerland, Denmark, Norway, and Sweden. Her next stop would be in Italy. Mary White, her daughter-in-law, accompanied her on this trip, while Ella again remained in Basel with Sara McEnterfer.

Mrs. White spent about three weeks in Italy, meeting speaking appointments, counseling with those who were experiencing difficulties, as well as dealing with those who were opposed to the preaching of the Advent message. Though they were glad for the time they could spend encouraging the believers in Italy, both she and Mary were happy to head for their temporary home in Basel.

In Basel Once Again

It was almost Christmas when they arrived back in Basel. Mary White was thrilled to be with Ella again. The day before Christmas a heavy snow blanketed the city. Ellen thought the large park in front of the publishing house was the most beautiful winter picture she had ever seen. As she walked in the park with Mary and Ella, she enjoyed little Ella's efforts to snowball her and her mother. Since she was only 4, they were in no danger. How they all enjoyed the cold, clear air and the sparkling snow!

When Willie returned to Basel in February from the General Conference session in Battle Creek, he brought Marian Davis with him. She would spend most of her time in Europe gathering and organizing Mrs. White's writings for *Spirit of Prophecy,* volume 1, dealing with Old

Testament history. This volume eventually became *Patriarchs and Prophets.*

Back at Home

In 1887, at the end of her two-year mission assignment in Europe, Ellen White returned to the United States. W. C. White still had some business to care for, and his wife, Mary, and two daughters, Ella and little Mabel, who had been born on November 1, 1886, sailed to America with his mother. Mary was becoming increasingly ill with symptoms of tuberculosis, and it was imperative that she reach Dr. Kellogg at Battle Creek Sanitarium as soon as possible. When they disembarked in New York, Ellen White went on to the New England camp meeting.

Mary and the little girls, accompanied by others who were arriving early to attend the General Conference session in November, went directly to Battle Creek. As soon as she arrived Mary had an appointment with Dr. John Harvey Kellogg. She was hospitalized immediately. She did indeed have tuberculosis.

After the camp meetings Ellen went to Healdsburg, where she planned to spend the winter. A grim cloud hovered over the family, for Mary wasn't improving as they had hoped. Mrs. White had occasion to visit in Burrough Valley, California, and after experiencing the mild climate there she thought it might be a good place for Mary to recuperate. Maybe she would get better there. With the help of Mrs. McOmber, Willie took Mary to Burrough Valley. After taking a camp meeting appointment in Nevada, Ellen went to Burrough Valley to be with Mary. She hoped she could spend a couple of months there, and perhaps do some writing.

But even Burrough Valley, beautiful as it was, didn't help their dear Mary recover her health. From there she was taken to Boulder, Colorado, but she continued to fail rapidly. At that point it was clear that she wouldn't live much longer. Willie was with her when she died on June 18, 1890, at the age of 33. Her little girls, Ella and Mabel, were 8 and 3.

Mary's short life had been busy and fruitful. She had been not only a wife and mother, but a writer, an editor, and a publishing house worker. Her funeral was held in the Battle Creek Tabernacle on June 25, and she rests in the family plot in Oak Hill Cemetery.

A True Daughter to Ellen White

Ellen White and her daughter-in-law Mary shared a deep love and affection for each other. Before her marriage to Willie White, Mary had worked at the Review and Herald in Battle Creek. After their marriage, Willie was asked to be the manager of the new publishing house, Pacific Press Publishing Association in Oakland, California. There Mary served as assistant to James White, who was the editor of the *Signs of the Times*. Her dedication to the cause of God, as well as her warm personality, endeared her to her in-laws. She and Ellen shared many good times, as well as difficult ones. Ellen often referred to her as "our dear Mary."

CHAPTER 4

Ellen G. White:
Part 2
The Salamanca Vision

Salamanca, New York, was the site of the Pennsylvania state meeting in 1890. Although she had a severe cold, Mrs. White met her speaking appointments. By Monday afternoon her head was so stuffy that she could barely stand on her feet, yet she felt the sustaining power of God upon her. She spoke of the need of faith, and of loving God supremely and our neighbor as ourselves. She couldn't remember anything she said, but others told her that "the power of God was upon you."

She wrote, "I knew that the words of the Lord Jesus had come to the people. Many spoke of the help they received from the words spoken. I told them to render no thanks to me. God . . . alone should have the praise. I was only an instrument in His hands."

Weary and sick, she tried to get back to the room where she was staying. But so many people kept stopping her to ask advice and counsel that it was more than an hour before she was able to close the door behind her.

Her diary record reveals that she knelt by her chair, disheartened by her pain, the journey, and the appointments ahead of her. But before she could speak a word in prayer the whole room seemed to be filled with a soft, silvery light, and her pain, disappointment, and discouragement disappeared. She was filled with comfort and hope as the peace of Christ washed over her. The presence of Jesus was in the room. Now she could better understand the meaning of Jacob's words when he said, "Surely the Lord is in this place; and I knew it not. . . . This is none other but the house of God, and this is the gate of heaven."

Heaven indeed seemed very near, and her heart was filled with joy and gladness. She didn't want to sleep; she wanted only to be with Jesus and feast on the heavenly manna. She wrote, "What a night that was to my soul! Every breath was prayer mingled with praise to God."

In vision that night God showed her a great number of things in regard to the publishing work. The next morning she didn't have time to write out what she had been shown in the vision, but she did enter the date of November 4 in her diary and wrote: "I longed to be where I could write out the things that were opened to me the past night." She left a blank space in the diary in order to fill in the account of the vision when she had time.

When W. C. White and A. T. Robinson came to her room the next morning, they expected to find her ill to the point of being forced to abandon the rest of the trip and return to Battle Creek. Instead, they found her beaming with joy and happiness, with no more weariness and despair. She had been healed and was ready to continue the journey to Virginia. She spoke briefly to them of her experience the night before, saying she wanted to tell them of some things that had been presented to her. Then she went on to talk about the rest of their trip, and nothing more was said of the previous evening. They were to continue on to Virginia that day.

In the space she had left marked "November 4" she later wrote of being in communion with God throughout the night. She seemed to be in different locations bearing testimonies of reproof and warning. In one scene she seemed to be in Battle Creek in an assembly of ministers and representatives of the Review and Herald office. There was a spirit of belligerence as plans were revealed and urged upon those in the meeting. The men seemed to be willing to approve tactics that not only were unwise, but were inspired by Satan himself. If the schemes were adopted, it would be a very bad situation and would bring no honor to God or His work.

Later, in several other places in her journal, she referred to the vision, but she was not able to write fully until she returned home to Battle Creek.

Arriving, by train, in Sands (now Stanley), Virginia, they had a few days to relax before the meetings began. One of the highlights there was a trip to Luray to see the famous caverns. She commented that "to give a description of this scene is simply impossible. It was wonderful, too wonderful to describe." They spent an hour and a half in the caverns, then had a leisurely drive back to their rooms in Sands.

Mrs. White spoke often at these meetings in Sands, and on Thursday night, November 20, she received another vision. When the meetings in

Virginia were finished, the little group moved on to meetings held in Brooklyn, New York. Several visions were given to her during this time that related to the one given at Salamanca, New York, earlier in the month. She referred to these visions in her journal during November and December, writing of things that had been shown her concerning the publishing work and the attitudes of those carrying responsibilities in that area.

A particular portion of the vision of November 3 made a vivid impression on Mrs. White's mind. That was the portion she had wanted to relate to W. C. White and A. T. Robinson. She wrote of it briefly in various places in her journal, then in more detail, probably while they were in Brooklyn.

The General Conference Session of 1891

Thursday, March 5, marked the opening of the 1891 General Conference session in Battle Creek. Ellen White was asked to meet with the participants in the early-morning sessions whenever she could. She made a point of being there each morning to give a talk. She wrote to friends that there were times when it was apparent that the Holy Spirit was present and working on hearts. Of the March 7 meeting Uriah Smith reported:

"Sister White spoke on the importance of preaching the Word, and the danger of covering up, and keeping in the background, the distinctive features of our faith, under the impression that prejudice will thereby be avoided. If there is committed to us a special message, as we believe, that message must go, without reference to the customs or prejudices of the world, not governed by a policy of fear or favor. Some will receive it and be sanctified through it, though multitudes will oppose and reject it. But it must go everywhere till the very earth is lighted with its glory."

A. T. Robinson, who had been in Salamanca at the time of the November 3, 1890, vision, noted a point in Mrs. White's talk that seemed significant to him. Three times she had attempted to report what she had been shown at Salamanca, but each time her thoughts seemed to veer off in another direction. The third time she had tried to refer to that meeting, she had spoken almost impatiently, "But I'll have more to say about that some other time."

Later that same Sabbath, March 7, Elder O. A. Olsen, General Conference president, asked Ellen White if she would be coming to the early-morning ministers' meeting on Sunday. She replied that she did not plan to be there; she had done her part, and she would leave the rest up to him. Olsen then planned that he and W. W. Prescott would lead out in the morning meeting.

However, early the next morning Mrs. White woke with the certainty that she was to go to the ministers' meeting and give the message that the Lord had given her about three months earlier in Salamanca, New York. As W. C. White and two others walked past his mother's home they saw lights in the house. Elder White said he would stop and see if his mother was ill. She was busily writing but told him that she had been awakened by an angel about 3:00 a.m. The angel told her to go to the meeting and relate the things shown to her in Salamanca. She had been writing for about two hours.

Willie White escorted his mother to the Tabernacle, where the meeting was already under way and the ministers were in a season of prayer. After the prayers were finished and a hymn had been sung, Elder Olsen saw Mrs. White sitting there with a bundle of manuscript in her arms. Since he had not expected her to be there, he was sure the Lord had given her something special for the meeting. He invited her to come forward, and she stated that the Lord had impressed her that it was now time for her to share some things that had been shown to her in November of the previous year.

In the vision on November 3, in Salamanca, her Guide had taken her to a council where certain men were gathered in a secret meeting. One held up a copy of the *American Sentinel,* a paper that supported the Sabbath, and said that the words "Seventh-day Adventist" should be dropped from the pages of the journal and nothing should be said about the Sabbath. Remarks were made contrary to the principles of faith held by Seventh-day Adventists, and it was urged that if these and other steps were taken, the influential men of the world would accept the magazine, it would become popular, and a greater work would be done through it. She went on to say that several visions had been given to her concerning the publishing work and the unconsecrated men who were in responsible positions in that area.

In the vision she had seen the men begin to work out a policy to make the *Sentinel* a worldly success by eliminating references to Seventh-day Adventists. She stated that this policy was the first of many wrong steps, and that principles taught in the *American Sentinel* were the "very sum and substance of the advocacy of the Sabbath."

Her words were startling to some of the men present that Sunday morning. At the close of her remarks Elder A. F. Ballenger rose to his feet. He told the group that he was in the meeting that had been held the night before until a very late hour, and that Mrs. White had described it just as it happened. He confessed that he was on the wrong side of the question, but now he was taking his position on the *right* side. Tears flowed from many eyes as confessions of wrong ideas and practices were made.

Ellen White was shocked. All this time she had thought that the meeting shown to her three months earlier had been held at that time!

Elder Robinson thought he would "never forget the look of perplexity on the face of the dear woman, as she looked at Brother Ballenger and exclaimed, 'Last night!' Others reported that she repeated in astonishment, 'Last night! Last night!' "

When Elder Ballenger took his seat, Clement Eldridge stood to speak. He said that after the close of the previous evening's meeting, some of the leaders met in his room at the Review office. They locked the door and discussed the matter that Mrs. White had just presented to them. He said that she had given a more accurate picture of the meeting than he himself could have given. He confessed that last night he thought he was right, but after hearing her testimony he could see that he was wrong.

Others who were in the meeting on Saturday night gave their confessions that it was a meeting that never should have been held. To a man they could see where they had been wrong.

O. A. Olsen, president of the General Conference, sat in "blank bewilderment." He didn't know what Mrs. White was talking about. He knew nothing of a secret meeting such as she had described.

One extant statement relative to this experience was signed by six prominent ministers and reads:

"The relation of this vision made a profound and solemn impression upon that large congregation of Seventh-day Adventist ministers present at that early-morning meeting. When they heard those who had been reproved for the wrong course taken in that council confess that all Mrs. White had said about them was true in every particular, they saw the seal of divine inspiration had been set upon that vision and testimony. The power and solemnity of that meeting made an impression upon the minds of those present not soon to be forgotten."

See *Ellen G. White: The Lonely Years,* pages 466-482, for further details on this experience.

Chapter 5

Ellen G. White:
Part 3
Australia Beckons

The year 1891 brought a rather urgent request from the General Conference officers that Ellen White spend some time in the new field of Australia. They felt it would be a great blessing to the cause there, and—if she had light in this direction—she was invited to sail for Australia that same autumn. It was understood that her son W. C. White would accompany her. For weeks she prayed for guidance and light on what she should do, but none was forthcoming. To make a move such as that would be a great sacrifice, but she would go in a heartbeat if she could be sure it was God's will.

However, despite her prayers, God was silent. She had no light to go or not to go.

At last she decided to go. She and W. C. White, along with several helpers and assistants, sailed from San Francisco on November 12, 1891. About 25 friends gathered to see them off. Elder and Mrs. G. B. Starr were already in Honolulu, waiting for them. The plan was that they would be away for about two years. With that in mind, Willie made a hard decision that he felt was in the best interest of his children: he would leave his young daughters, Ella and Mabel, in the care of Miss Mary Mortensen, in his own home in Battle Creek.

Ellen had barely begun to get her "land legs" after arriving in Australia when she began to experience the first onset of symptoms that proved to be a severe and debilitating illness. Despite that, the conference session was in progress, and she was put to work immediately. She not only met several speaking appointments, but also counseled with individuals and committees. Meanwhile, she and her traveling companions needed a place to stay, and house hunting became the main item of concern.

In Preston they found a nice brick house with nine rooms. It was a little small for seven adults, but they could make it work. They rented the unfurnished house for six months and spent the next couple of days buying used furniture and other necessary household items. The house was five miles from the city, so it was necessary to buy a horse and carriage. Her helpers soon got the yard and garden in shape. With some extra water, the flowers grew and thrived, and Mrs. White was delighted with them, writing: "Dahlias, the richest beauties, are in full bloom, and fuchsias flourish. I never saw them blossom as they do here; the geraniums, Lady Washingtons, in immense bunches of the richest colors to delight the eye."

As for Ellen herself, she had begun to feel quite ill during the conference session. Her pain intensified, and she was becoming increasingly limited in her activities. About the time she became ill, she wrote to S. N. Haskell, "I am now writing on the life of Christ, and I have had a great comfort and blessing in my writing. It may be I am a cripple in order to do this work so long neglected."

Her sickness was a severe attack of what probably was rheumatoid arthritis, the same illness from which her twin sister suffered. Each week found her in more pain. Still, she kept writing. She was impatient with her feebleness. She had come to Australia as the Lord's messenger, to minister to the people. How could she do this when such prolonged misery limited her physical activities?

Eventually she began to see the suffering as part of God's plan. She remembered that not once had God failed her. She began to realize that precious experiences had run like "threads of gold" all through this severe affliction.

Speaking of her work on the manuscript about the life of Christ, she wrote to O. A. Olsen, president of the General Conference, in Battle Creek, "I tremble for fear lest I shall belittle the great plan of salvation by cheap words."

As her illness worsened, she couldn't lift her feet from the floor without great agony, and her hips and lower back ached and throbbed sharply. Her right arm, from the elbow down, was the only part of her body that was free from pain. She couldn't lie down for more than two hours at a time; then she must be moved to another position. The doctors said she would never walk again. But Ellen White had been endowed from childhood with a generous measure of perseverance. It showed up again and again throughout her life. When things seemed impossible, she kept trying till she achieved her goal.

To make it possible for her to write, her helpers bolstered her chair with pillows. They fixed up a padded writing frame on which she could rest her arms, with a rubber pillow under them. In this way she could write on a hard surface on her lap. Sometimes she could write like this for a couple of hours before needing to change positions. All this was done while she was in the most intense pain.

Despite her illness and suffering, she still found ways to fulfill her dream of bearing the testimonies given her by God for the people of Australia. She also had messages of counsel to write for individuals and institutions as the Lord gave her light. As a result, writing on the life of Christ made slow progress.

In 1892, after many months of affliction, during which she and her caregivers did everything they knew to bring about healing, Ellen White asked to be anointed. It was during this quiet time of meditation about praying for the sick that she wrote what probably was the basis for the chapter entitled "Prayer for the Sick" in *The Ministry of Healing*.

On May 20, 1892, Elder and Mrs. A. G. Daniells, Elder and Mrs. G. C. Tenney, and Brothers Stockton and Smith came to her home for an anointing service. It was a special time for all of them as they gathered around Mrs. White's chair and earnestly prayed for her healing.

She was "relieved, but not restored," and she now was content to wait for the Lord to work in her behalf.

Her illness began to subside, and although it was a slow recovery, she was able to get around more easily, and gradually began to take up her work again. That meant more traveling, speaking, and committee meetings, but not much writing.

The Search for a School Property

It was in late December 1893 when the search for suitable property for a school began in earnest. They wanted a large parcel of land, with good soil, at a cheap price. Because of the economic depression in America, both Mrs. White's wages and those of W. C. White had been cut, and funds were hard to come by.

Many were the prayers for the right location at the right price—and for generous donors to make the proposed school a reality. They needed fertile land that would grow good crops to support the school family. W. C. White wrote to his friend C. H. Jones at the Pacific Press: "We're planning to buy a large tract of land, and we can scarcely get enough money to go and see it."

Several locations were inspected, but it was the Brettville estate on Dora Creek that best fit their needs and their pocketbook. Nearly 1,500 acres could be had for $4,500. A contract was signed and a small fee paid to hold the land until the property could be more closely inspected by workers from Melbourne.

As the result of an appeal by Ellen White published on the back page of the Review, the L. N. Lawrence family, at their own expense, moved from Michigan to Australia to help in whatever way they could with the new work there. They rented a small house in Dora Creek, and when church leaders came to look at the land, the Lawrences provided a place for them to stay. The next week Ellen White joined the group. She couldn't wait to see what was going on.

Although called a creek, Dora Creek was more of a narrow, deep river bordering the Brettville estate. Preliminary inspection of the property had been quite favorable. Now there was a "fly in the ointment" in the form of a government expert, Mr. A. H. Benson, who had examined the land at their request. He reported it to be "very poor, sour, sandy loam resting on yellow clay, or very poor swamp covered with different species of Melaleuca." The entire property was "sour, requiring liming and draining."

To reinforce his disdain of what he considered to be poor, unfertile soil, he also remarked, "If a bandicoot [a small animal about the size of a rabbit] were to cross the tract of land, he would find it necessary to carry his lunch with him."

But Ellen White didn't agree. She couldn't see how land that could grow trees the size of those on the property could be of poor quality. As the others in the scouting party walked over the land, she sat on a log planning what could be done. She saw nothing discouraging in the purchase of the property. The men returned from their expedition with much better impressions than they'd had before. They felt that some of the land was better than anything they'd seen elsewhere, and it met with their favor.

Far into the night the committee discussed the whole venture, and most of them felt this was the right place. They also were aware of Mrs. White's positive attitude toward the potential of the place. Late that night they voted to make the purchase for $4,500.

Even though the vote had been taken, they wanted to take another day to explore a little further—just to be on the safe side. That morning, before leaving the cottage where they were staying at Dora Creek, they knelt together to ask for divine guidance. Ellen White felt impressed to ask God for some kind of special token or evidence that would show them all that they were following His leading.

With them was Elder Stephen McCullagh, who had a lung and throat disease. He was steadily getting worse, and there seemed to be no help for him. Mrs. White wrote to O. A. Olsen of the experience:

"While we were all bowed in prayer, the Lord rolled upon me the burden of prayer for Brother McCullagh, that he should be blessed, strengthened, and healed. It was a most blessed season, and Brother McCullagh says the difficulty has been removed from his throat, and he has been gaining ever since."

Speaking of the experience later, Elder McCullagh said that it seemed as if a shock of electricity went through his body. His coughing ceased, and he soon regained his normal weight and strength. Thirty-four years later he was still living.

As they walked the property that Thursday, the committee members were convinced that the Brettville estate was the place for the new school.

Prayer continued that if it was indeed the right place, obstacles would be removed and the way made clear. A contract was signed and a down payment made. In another month they had to make a payment of $1,400. The balance was due in two years—or they could pay in entirety at any time.

The Land

Stephen Belden had been married to Ellen White's sister Sarah, who died of tuberculosis in 1868. He was remarried, and he and his wife were doing self-supporting mission work in Australia. Ellen met him again soon after her arrival in Sydney. As she and the men discussed how the land could be improved and good crops grown, Ellen cited Stephen as a man who "plowed a piece of land, and worked the soil thoroughly, and raised a most profitable crop of sweet corn for the school."

There were many who told Stephen that it would be a waste of time to try to grow anything in that soil and that he shouldn't even bother with it, but he was determined to show them what could be done. He volunteered to come to the school property at the right season and teach them how to work the land.

The more Ellen saw of the land, the more amazed she was at the low price they had paid. In her mind's eye she saw alfalfa fields, strawberry patches, fields of sweet corn. Over there, she imagined, that ground would raise good potatoes; and all kinds of fruit would flourish just over that little rise. She had it all laid out in her mind. She wrote about special light that had been presented to her on several occasions: "Words were spoken of land which I was looking at," she wrote, "and after deep plowing and thorough cultivating, it brought forth a bountiful harvest. Having had this matter presented to me at different times, I am more than ever convinced that this is the right location for the school."

Yet another experience further confirmed the location:

"Before I visited Cooranbong, the Lord gave me a dream. In my dream I was taken to the land that was for sale in Cooranbong. Several of our brethren had been solicited to visit the land, and I dreamed that I was walking upon the ground. I came to a neat-cut furrow that had been plowed one quarter of a yard deep and two yards in length. Two of the brethren who had been acquainted with the rich soil of Iowa were standing before the furrow and saying, 'This is not good land; the soil is not favorable.' But One who has often spoken in counsel . . . said, 'False witness has been borne of this land.'"

The next day as Mrs. White was walking over some of the property, she saw a plowed furrow, just as he had seen in the dream. There were two men there and they spoke the same critical words she'd heard in the dream.

The School Plans Become Reality

There were ups and downs, successes and setbacks as building progressed, but on April 28, 1897, the Avondale School for Christian Workers opened—literally hewn out of the forest. The corner brick of the first building, Bethel Hall, was laid by Ellen White on October 5, 1896. The school opened with 10 students and four teachers. By the close of the first term 60 students called it their school.

In 1911 the name was changed to Australasian Missionary College; in 1964 it was changed to Avondale College. And the rest, as the saying goes, is history.

The Desire of Ages Comes to Fruition

In the late summer of 1897 Marian Davis wrote to Willie White, "Sister White seems inclined to write, and I have no doubt she will bring out many precious things. I hope . . . to get them into the book. There is one thing, however, that not even the most competent editor could do—that is, to prepare the manuscript before it is written."

Ellen White penned a poignant note in her diary in 1897: "In writing upon the life of Christ I am deeply wrought upon. I forget to breathe as I should. I cannot endure the intensity of feeling that comes over me as I think of what Christ has suffered in our world."

About the end of March 1898 the last of the manuscript was sent to the publisher. All through the years the project had been known as the Life of Christ, and it was supposed that would be the title.

However, suggestions began to come from various individuals in both Australia and America. W. C. White said he didn't want to say much about the title, but some titles, he felt, were "a hundred miles nearer being appropriate than the best of the others that have been recommended to us." In other words, even some of the best ones weren't all that great!

The publishers narrowed their list down to The Desire of All Nations and The Desire of Ages, both based on Haggai 2:7, "The desire of all nations shall come." After much consideration the title was chosen. It would be *The Desire of Ages*.

Sometimes authors receive the first copy of their book that comes off the press. But in this case Ellen White didn't get the first copy. A young pressman, Roy Bernard, was in charge of the press on which the book was printed. Roy was engaged to a young woman by the name of Minnie Hunter. He thought the first copy of *The Desire of Ages* would make a very special engagement gift for a very special girl—his Minnie. When the first copy rolled off Roy's press, he tracked it all the way through to the binding process. As the bound copy came from the binding machine Roy caught it and rushed to the business office to pay for his beloved's gift.

That night Roy presented the first copy of the first edition of *The Desire of Ages* to his future wife.

Of course, Ellen White received one of the first copies. Figuratively speaking, bells rang and whistles blew as she held the new book to her heart, savoring the smell of printer's ink and new leather. At last the book on the life of Christ had come to fruition. She held the volume close to her heart for a few moments before opening its covers, remembering all the long years it had taken to reach this important moment.

Her mind went back to 1858 when she had written volume 1 of *Spiritual Gifts,* the first writing of her great controversy vision. Of the 219 pages in that first little book, more than 50 of them centered on Christ. In 1876 and 1877 Ellen White rewrote and enlarged her narrative of Christ's life and work so that it comprised more than 640 pages in *Spirit of Prophecy,* volumes 2 and 3. Then in the 1890s she expanded the account still further. Now she held in her hands the end result of all those years of labor. It has been cited as one of the most beautiful books—if not the most beautiful—ever written on the life of Christ.

First Camp Meeting in Australia

There came another first for the mission field of Australia—the first camp meeting. Scheduled to open on Friday, January 5, 1894, at Brighton, it looked to be a big one. There were so many calls for reservations that the committee had to buy and rent dozens more tents than they had planned for. When Mrs. White arrived, there were more than 100 tents, housing 500 people. Interest and enthusiasm were unprecedented.

The careful, orderly arrangement of the tents and grounds impressed the many non-Adventist visitors who flocked to the meetings. They crowded into the main tent to hear Ellen White speak on such topics as the Ten Commandments, Sabbathkeeping, and the second coming of Christ.

But not everybody appreciated the meetings. Several juvenile delinquents—called larrikins in Australia—committed acts of vandalism and mischief, even pulling down one of the tents. Guards kept the damage to a minimum. It seemed to these hoodlums that Mrs. White was the most prominent person there, and they didn't like prominent or important people. Plotting to pull one of their clever tricks on her, they decided it would be a good joke to pull her tent down—with her in it.

Unfortunately for them, one of the gang boasted about their plan. Word leaked out to those in charge, and the police were called. The city sent out a tall, heavy-set, Irish Catholic policeman to guard Mrs. White's tent.

She had heard about the plan, but she wasn't worried about what might happen. Angels had protected her many times from accident, violence, and hatred, and she didn't see any reason to be afraid now. But to please those who were concerned for her safety, she accepted the policeman's presence outside her tent.

He patrolled the area, watching for the troublemakers, but the boys never showed up. Some of the younger camp guards had warned the gang members not to try anything because the city had sent a law officer.

Back and forth he walked, keeping a watchful eye. A little past midnight he thought he caught a glimpse of something out of the corner of his eye, but decided it was his imagination, for he saw nothing amiss. Darkness shrouded the tent as it stood peacefully in the midst of the trees.

Just as he began to turn toward another part of the campground he suddenly saw a beam of light hovering over Mrs. White's tent. Gripping his nightstick tightly, he watched as gradually the light assumed the shape of an angel. His reaction was automatic—he dropped to his knees and crossed himself.

Awestruck, the Irish Catholic officer watched the angel for several minutes, then slowly rose and walked away. Mrs. White didn't need his protection. God was protecting her very well without his assistance. Reporting back to the station house, he found his story accepted without question.

The police officer wanted to see this woman who was guarded by an angel; he wanted to hear what she had to say. The next day he went back to the campground, and in the big tent he heard such preaching as he'd never experienced before. And the more he heard, the more interested he became.

He accepted Jesus as his Savior and was baptized. No doubt God allowed the officer to see the angel because He knew that this was the key to creating an interest in the gospel. The converted man resigned from the force and moved to a nearby village, where he became an active lay member in the church. His witness for his Savior was so outstanding that many others also found a new life in Christ.

A Newcomer Enters the Picture

One of Ellen White's helpers, her niece May Walling, found it necessary to return to America. Willie suggested to his mother, who was spending some time in Granville, New South Wales, that she might want to consider Miss May Lacey as a replacement for May Walling. Mrs. White was favorably impressed during her interview with the young woman, and Miss Lacey returned to Cooranbong with her. Mrs. White felt that May Lacey "filled the bill nicely" as her companion.

Willie White's mother soon learned why he was so eager to have Miss Lacey on her staff. He had met May at the Bible school in Melbourne and was quite taken with her. Their friendship eventually developed to the point of marriage, and Ellen was as pleased as Willie at the prospect. The wedding would take place in May's home in Tasmania. She had been born in India, near Calcutta, where her father was British police commissioner. Since his retirement, the family had made their home in Tasmania. Literature evangelists had brought the good news of salvation to them, and the entire family had joined the church.

The wedding was held in the home of the bride, with about 20 friends and family present. Mr. Palfryman, a Methodist minister and an old friend of the Lacey family, conducted the ceremony, and Mrs. White offered the prayer of commitment and consecration.

After the wedding supper, the bride finished packing and her husband went to a committee meeting! Later in the evening they boarded a train headed for Launceston, where they met with 17 newly baptized Sabbathkeepers.

Meanwhile, Willie had sent for his two girls, now ages 13 and 8, who were still in Battle Creek. It was a happy reunion between Willie and his girls, and they were warmly welcomed to Australia, where they would spend the next five years. Upon meeting their new mother, they promptly fell in love with her. Mabel summed up their feelings:

"When I heard Father was to marry one only 21 years old, I thought I should see a little bit of a woman. But I didn't expect to see such a tall, large woman. And I just said to myself, 'Father has picked out just the one I can love and respect.'"

And May was just as pleased with the two girls.

A year later identical twin boys were born to Willie and May. Ellen

White was given the privilege of naming them: Herbert Clarence and James Henry. When they were about 8 months old, the family moved out to Cooranbong and lived temporarily in a little house back of Ellen White's home, Sunnyside. Willie was building a house across the road.

It didn't take the boys, Henry and Herbert, long to figure out that when Grandma's buggy came to their porch, it meant a ride down the road. Ellen describes one incident:

"They are in such ecstasies over getting a chance to ride that I have not the heart to say no. So they bundle in with their little red coats and white plush caps. We are all caught in the mistake of not distinguishing them one from the other."

Chapter 6

Ellen G. White:

Part 4
Needed Back in America

The years in Australia were busy and productive, with all kinds of progress in the work of God. As 1900 opened, Mrs. White, 72, had no plans to return to America. She wrote to Edson telling him that she had sent for some large volumes of Barnes' notes on the Bible that were supposed to be in her house in Battle Creek. The house had been sold, and she wanted her best books sent to her.

It was in Australia that God told her to "gather up the fragments that nothing be lost." It had been repeated to her several times. But it wasn't until Sarah Peck, who had been a teacher in South Africa, came on the scene that some semblance of order began to emerge. Sarah sorted, read, filed, and indexed Ellen White's manuscripts. This was the basis for the letter and manuscript files that exist today in the White Estate vault.

Although early in January Ellen had no thought of returning to America, by March she was overwhelmed with the conviction that she was "needed in America." Struggle as she would against the conviction, it remained: her testimony was needed in America now. Plans were made to sail in August.

Ellen White sold her house and land, with furniture, farming implements, and livestock, to a family who wanted to be near the school. Willie exchanged property with Metcalf Hare, and then sold the place to the school. They gave God all the credit for arranging the easy disposal of their properties. It was Willie's firm opinion that once they reached America, under no circumstances should they locate in Battle Creek or anywhere else east of the Rocky Mountains.

Ellen's traveling party would include her four assistants—Sara McEnterfer, Marian Davis, Sarah Peck, and Maggie Hare—and Willie's family, which now numbered seven: Willie, his wife, May; his two oldest daughters, Ella, 18, and Mabel, 13; the twins, Henry and Herbert, 4; and the new baby, Grace, 3 months.

A farewell service was held in the Avondale church for all of them on Sunday afternoon, August 26. Speeches and well wishes were given, and two autograph books, beautifully bound in blue velvet, were presented to Mrs. White. There was a page for every day of the voyage, each filled with poems, drawings, and messages of love and encouragement.

Nine busy years had come to a close. Before them lay a 23-day journey of 7,200 miles across the Pacific. Three stops would relieve the monotony as the ship plowed across the waters—New Zealand, Samoa, and the Hawaiian Islands.

A Stop in Samoa

In Samoa the passengers had a chance to go ashore. There was one little problem: the ship had to anchor at a distance, and the small boat that took them from the ship to the shore couldn't go all the way to the beach because of the shallow water. Native men waded out to help the women ashore, carrying them to keep their long dresses from getting wet.

Two of the men locked their hands together and made a chair with their arms for Mrs. White. They carried her, safe and dry, to the beach, where she sat on a large rock.

Another native man took 4-month-old Grace in his arms and held an umbrella over her, shielding her from the hot sun. Then he motioned for May White to get on his back. She somehow scrambled onto his back, wrapped her arms and legs around him, and off they went toward the shore, her full skirts billowing about her. It was such a funny sight that Ellen White laughed so hard she fell off the rock.

At Home in St. Helena

Once they arrived in San Francisco, Mrs. White was eager to get settled and begin her work. She discovered that Oakland had grown and changed a great deal during the time she'd been gone. Sabbath and Sunday were spent with friends, and on Monday she began house hunting. Ellen claimed the Lord's promise that He would provide just the right place for her. After a few days Willie suggested to his mother that she and Sara

McEnterfer go to the St. Helena Sanitarium for a little rest and he would continue to search for a house.

At the sanitarium, where they were well cared for, conversation turned to the frustration of hunting for suitable housing. Someone mentioned that a house just "under the hill" was for sale.

The next morning, Friday, Ellen White went down to see the "place under the hill." It was a large Victorian house built by Robert Pratt. In the past she had often admired it as she passed by.

She was delighted. This home would meet her every need. The house stood on a knoll, with an orchard and vineyard, a garden, and a hayfield. The house itself was well constructed, had seven rooms, and was completely furnished, from dishes right down to carpets on the floor. Also included were wagons, carriages, and horses. During the ocean crossing God had assured her of "a haven of rest," and surely this was it. The house with all its furnishings could be hers for less than she received for her home in Australia.

On Sunday morning she couldn't resist going down the hill to take another look at the Pratt place. She could only conclude, "This place was none of my seeking. It has come to me without a thought or purpose of mine. The Lord is so kind and gracious to me. I can trust my interests with Him who is too wise to err and too good to do me harm."

Details were settled, and Ellen and her family of assistants moved in. Willie and his family lived in a nearby cottage. She had brought only one piece of furniture with her from Australia—her comfortable writing chair, with the writing board that could be swung to one side for easy movement.

She gave Willie a portion of the property on which to build a house. Some of the land went for a church school and another plot for a food factory.

Her home in Australia had been called Sunnyside. Now she needed a name for her new home. Since there were large elms in front of the house, Willie tried Shady Elms, but it didn't catch on. He used it only once, and no one else used it at all. A few days later someone came up with Elmshaven, and that became the name of the "house under the hill." It was to be her home for the next 15 years.

The 1901 General Conference Session

Busy days sped by, filled with many and varied projects and activities.

Suddenly it was time to head east for Battle Creek and the 1901 General Conference session.

Mrs. White's main burden at the session was to call for the reorganization of the General Conference. The work was growing throughout the world, and it was time for a wider distribution of the responsibilities that had been carried by a few persons at the headquarters office. It took several days to map out all the changes that needed to be made, but there was a good spirit, and no one became bitter or angry. Great and sweeping decisions were made in the best interests of the church as a whole.

Back Home at Elmshaven

After a long absence attending the 1901 session, Ellen White was glad to be back home at Elmshaven. She found her grapevines loaded with fruit; but there wasn't even one prune on any of the 2,000 trees. The buds had frozen in the April frost. It represented quite a financial loss to her, and since there was nothing she could do about it she tried to look on the bright side: "I thank the Lord that we shall not have the trouble and care of gathering the prunes!"

The Review and Herald

Over the years the Review and Herald Publishing Association had grown by leaps and bounds. By 1899 the floor space was 80,000 square feet, with up-to-date machinery in all departments. The West Building housed not only some departments of the publishing house but offices of the General Conference as well. The Review and Herald was the largest and most complete printing establishment in the state of Michigan.

In spite of all that, there were times of financial difficulty. In order to pay the bills, the management increased their commercial printing work, and some of it was damaging to the spiritual life of the workers through whose hands it passed.

Late in 1901 Ellen White wrote a testimony of warning to the Review and Herald board of directors. She told them that they were publishing inappropriate commercial material that was directly against the teachings of the Seventh-day Adventist Church, and the Lord was not pleased. The letter contained a significant sentence: "I have been almost afraid to open the *Review,* fearing to see that God has cleansed the publishing house by fire."

On Tuesday evening, December 30, 1902, that fear became a reality.

The bell in the cupola of the Dime Tabernacle rang twice, the signal that it was almost time for prayer meeting to begin. About the same time, the electricity went off. Looking out the window, Elder A. G. Daniells saw flames coming from the publishing house. Suddenly the fire alarm began to clang farther downtown, and a shout came over the frosty air: "The Review and Herald is on fire!"

By the time Daniells, president of the General Conference, and I. H. Evans, president and general manager of the publishing house, ran from the West Building, the pressroom was in flames. Within minutes the firefighters were there, pouring water onto the raging flames; but they were beyond control. The fire was moving so rapidly that they could only try to keep it from reaching other buildings and homes.

In the general excitement and panic Freddie Roberts, an artist, ran from the building with some of his materials, while Mr. McReynolds, a stenographer, ran out shouting that he had managed to slam the safe door shut. The night watchman was able to crawl from an upstairs window and down the fire escape ladder. The man was so panic-stricken, and his words tumbled out so fast and disjointed, that he could hardly be understood.

The firefighters hoped they could save the row of homes to the east of the burning building, and gradually the wind did shift so that the smoke and embers were blown across the park, away from the homes. An office worker in the West Building threw important General Conference papers into the vault and twirled the combination lock. Then he climbed onto the roof and guided firefighters as they sprayed water on the West Building, for it began to smoke here and there.

The flames roared like a freight train, and windows in the main building shattered from the heat. Equipment could be heard crashing through the floors, and within a half hour the roof had caved in. By this time hundreds of townspeople stood open-mouthed on the sidelines. The night sky glowed an eerie red as the brick walls fell into the flaming ruins.

Because the insurance was due to be renewed very soon, that very day the fire inspector had made his rounds throughout the building, examining wiring and other sources of possible danger. He had reported everything in good shape.

Some of the board members who watched the flames remembered

what Ellen White had written a little more than a year before.

Out in California, that Tuesday night had been a restless one for Ellen White. She had slept little, and in a vision she had anguished over the situation in Battle Creek. When she came down for breakfast the next morning, Sara McEnterfer told her the bad news that had come by telephone from C. H. Jones, manager of the Pacific Press. Mrs. White was shocked but not surprised. Only a few days earlier she had seen in vision a sword of fire over Battle Creek, "turning first in one direction and then in another." The Battle Creek Sanitarium had burned in February, and now the Review and Herald had suffered the same fate.

Months of decision-making followed the fire. One immediate and important decision was to discontinue commercial printing. The fire also had brought reality to the counsel Mrs. White had given as far back as the mid-1880s that there was danger in centering so many institutions in Battle Creek.

At the General Conference session of 1903, after the fire, she was very specific: "Let the General Conference offices and the publishing work be moved from Battle Creek. . . . Never lay a stone or brick in Battle Creek to rebuild the Review office there. God has a better place for it."

Both the General Conference and the Review and Herald moved to Takoma Park, Maryland, in 1903, and the following year Mrs. White spent five months there. The new work was getting started, and as part of the medical work the Washington Sanitarium and Hospital was under construction.

The General Conference Session of 1909

Through the years at Elmshaven Ellen White continued to write and publish, give counsel to individuals, churches, and committees, and meet speaking appointments. The last General Conference session she attended was in 1909 in Takoma Park, when she was 82. A large tent had been pitched on the grounds of Washington Missionary College. On three of the four Sabbaths of the session Ellen White gave the 11:00 sermon.

The first Sabbath that she spoke, the daily *Bulletin* reported that it "was a day long to be remembered" as the "aged servant of God" stood in that large tent to speak to more than a thousand people. There was no public address system, yet she was heard clearly and distinctly by everyone present.

One young minister tested it for himself. This was the first General Conference session that A. V. Olson had ever attended. He sat on the front row and heard Mrs. White so clearly that he moved to the back of the tent, where he heard just as well. Going outside and away from the tent, he still clearly heard her every word. Yet the Lord's messenger didn't shout. She spoke with a steady low voice supported by her abdominal muscles, as she had been instructed by God. No one had to strain to hear and understand her words.

Her last sermon was at the closing meeting on Sunday afternoon. Her topic was "Partakers of the Divine Nature." She urged that all move forward in the strength of God, remembering the heavenly kingdom that waits for His people. She reminded her hearers that angels of God were right there to keep them from sin, and that by faith each one could lay hold of divine power.

This was not only her last sermon at that session, but also the last sermon she would preach at any General Conference session. She took a step or two away from the pulpit, then turned back, picked up the Bible she had been reading from, and holding it out on hands that were unsteady with age, she exhorted, "Brethren and sisters, I commend unto you this Book."

These were her last words to the leaders of the church as they officially met in conference. She upheld the Word of God that had been so precious to her, the Word that she ever kept before the church and the world.

The Days Grow Shorter

Back at home in California, Mrs. White kept up her writing and preaching schedule, traveling often to southern California to meet appointments there.

On Thanksgiving Day, November 26, 1914, Ellen White turned 87. A few days earlier she had received a birthday present from an old friend, Mrs. F. H. DeVinney. She and her husband were missionaries in Japan. Mrs. DeVinney sent Ellen a beautiful hand-knit vest known as a "hug-me-tight," to keep her warm on chilly days. When Mrs. White tried it on, it came somewhat short of meeting in the middle. But she hadn't lost her sense of humor, for she instructed her secretary, Dores Robinson, to "thank Sister DeVinney for her gift, but tell her there's a great deal more to Sister White than some people think."

On Sabbath, February 13, 1915, as Mrs. White was entering her writing room, she fell and broke her hip. She was taken to St. Helena

Sanitarium for X-rays. Whether she fell and broke her hip, or whether her hip broke and she fell, at that time there was little that could be done for such a break. It was thought she would be more comfortable in her own home, and Dr. Klingerman sent a hospital bed down to Elmshaven so she could rest more comfortably. She never walked again, but on good days she was taken in a wheelchair to the little balcony where she enjoyed the sunshine and fresh air.

As the days and weeks went by, her appetite lagged and she grew weaker. One day as Sara McEnterfer was trying to entice her into eating, she remarked, "Well, Sara, I wouldn't want to die before my time by overeating." At least she hadn't lost her sense of humor.

Her strength continued to decline, and in early July she told Sara, "I don't suffer much, thank the Lord. It won't be long now."

Often the family gathered in her writing room on Sabbath for sundown worship. On one Sabbath, not long before her death, someone began to sing "There's a Land That Is Fairer Than Day." The others began to join in, and then they noticed that Mrs. White was singing, in a barely audible whisper, "'We shall sing on that beautiful shore the melodious songs of the blest, and our spirits shall sorrow no more, not a sigh for the blessing of rest.'"

It seemed that she was singing with the angel choir. A few days later she spoke her last words to her son W. C. White: "I know in whom I have believed."

On Friday, July 16, the nurse could see that the end was near, and she sent for Willie and May. They in turn sent for others, so that when Ellen White breathed her last she was surrounded by her family and friends. Willie described it as "like the burning out of a candle, so quiet."

Her neighbors in the Napa Valley remembered her as "the little white-haired lady who always spoke so lovingly of Jesus."

Final Cross-Continent Trip

Three funeral services were held for Ellen White. The first was on the lawn at Elmshaven; the second was at the camp meeting being held at Richmond, California; and the third was at the Tabernacle in Battle Creek.

The Battle Creek funeral was held at 11:00 a.m. on Sabbath, July 24. Many of the Michigan churches canceled their services so the members could attend. Local newspapers estimated that 3,500 people crowded into the Tabernacle, with 1,000 more standing quietly outside. It was the largest funeral that had ever been held in Battle Creek.

The simple black casket was placed directly in front of the pulpit, with an honor guard standing at the head and the foot of the bier. The guard was composed of six ministers, who alternated in pairs every 20 minutes. The funeral sermon was preached by S. N. Haskell, and the life sketch was read by A. G. Daniells. Both were friends and fellow workers from the early years of the Advent message.

Dudley M. Canright, who had bitterly opposed Mrs. White's work since his apostasy 28 years earlier, was there with his brother Jasper, a faithful Adventist. Both of these men were so moved that they went through the viewing line twice. The second time, Dudley Canright put his hand on the casket and with tears flowing down his face declared, "There is a noble Christian woman gone."

At the close of the service in the Tabernacle, the crowd moved out to Oak Hill Cemetery. The *Enquirer* described the scene: "Thousands followed the hearse to the cemetery. For this purpose every carriage in the city was used, and there were a number of automobiles. And then besides this, there were nine streetcars. No fares were collected on these cars, as they were provided by the church."

The graveside service was brief. A double quartet sang, scriptures were read, and a prayer was offered. Ellen White was buried next to her beloved husband, Elder James White, who had died in 1881. One day soon their experience of looking for their Lord will become a reality. Then they'll actually "see their Lord a-coming" and "hear the band of music" by the heavenly angels who escort them to the King of kings.

Their works do follow them.

Vignettes

A rather interesting legend has grown up around a purported statement that the Library of Congress considers *The Desire of Ages* to be the best book available on the life of Christ. The facts are these: For many years a Seventh-day Adventist was employed at the book desk at the Library of Congress. He was asked which five books he considered as being the best on the life of Christ.

He stated that his preference would be guided by what he wanted to learn from the book, or books, to be read. He put *The Desire of Ages* first on the list for spiritual discernment and practical application. He then listed four other volumes that he would select for various other reasons. He ended his statement by saying, "I will say that *The Desire of Ages* is well thought of in the Library of Congress."

The Desire of Ages has been translated into more than 50 languages. Millions of copies have been printed and distributed throughout the world. Only the heavenly records will reveal how many lives have been blessed and changed by reading this book.

Ellen White wrote that "God would be pleased to see *The Desire of Ages* in every home. In this book is contained the light He has given upon His word. To our [people] I would say, Go forth with your hearts softened and subdued by reading of the life of Christ."

⌢

Mrs. White wrote many books of counsel and help for those who want to live close to Jesus. All her writings are kept at the Ellen G. White Estate, at the General Conference headquarters in Silver Spring, Maryland. Visitors can see the 120 drawers of original manuscripts, the many books she wrote, and the big Bible that, while in vision, she held in one hand.

Ellen White faithfully served the Lord as His messenger for more than 70 years. In order to establish the church on a firm foundation, and to direct its leaders and members in their Christian lives, God gave Ellen White numerous dreams and visions, giving guidance and instruction to carry them through to His kingdom.

More than anything else, Mrs. White dreaded having visions that would require her to give unwelcome counsel to someone. The burden was very heavy and hard to bear. "If I could have my choice and please God as well, I would rather die than have a vision," she once said, "for every vision places me under great responsibility to bear testimonies of reproof and of warning, which has ever been against my feelings, causing me affliction of soul that is inexpressible. Never have I coveted my position, and yet I dare not resist the Spirit of God and seek an easier position."

From the Vermont camp meeting in 1880 she wrote to her son Willie, "I had some very bad, bad jobs to perform. I took Brother Bean and wife and talked to them very plainly. They did not rise up against it. I cried myself; could not help it."

For more than 30 years the White Estate office has been trying to make clear that the following statement has been falsely attributed to Ellen White. She did not write it. In spite of everything, it keeps popping up here and there.

"Prayer is the answer to every problem in life. . . . No mind is so dull that it cannot be made brilliant," etc. It has been given various references, one of which is *Review and Herald,* October 7, 1865. The statement actually does appear in the *Review and Herald* of October 7, 1965, in an article by R. A. Rentfro. He says that "someone has said" the above statement. Someone apparently did say it, but that someone was not Ellen White, nor did Rentfro say it was.

For further apocryphal statements, see *Index to the Writings of Ellen G. White,* Appendix C, or log on to the White Estate Web site at WhiteEstate.org.

Grace White Jacques, granddaughter of Ellen White, told the story of General Conference president A. G. Daniells coming to visit her grandmother at Elmshaven. He was admitted at the front door and invited to go right on upstairs to Mrs. White's writing room. He went up the curved staircase, admiring the view from the stained-glass window on the landing, and on down the hallway. As he entered her writing room, she greeted him and then said, "Did you see the angel?"

With an astonished look he replied that he hadn't.

Surprised, she said, "Why, you passed him there in the hallway, just as you stepped through the door."

A. G. Daniells may have been president of the General Conference, but no doubt even he was more than a little startled by this calm announcement.

Chapter 7

Frederick Wheeler: First Ordained Minister to Preach the Sabbath

My brother, you'd do better to set that Communion table back against the wall and cover it with the white cloth until you're willing to keep all the commandments of God yourself!

So thought Mrs. Rachel Oakes as she sat in church one Sunday morning. In fact, she could hardly restrain her urge to jump up during the meeting and tell Pastor Frederick Wheeler just that.

Mrs. Oakes was visiting her daughter, Delight, a schoolteacher in Washington, New Hampshire, and had come to church with her that Sunday morning.

Frederick Wheeler is best known in Adventist circles for becoming the first Sabbathkeeping Adventist minister. But that hadn't happened yet, and on this Sunday morning as he conducted the celebration of the Lord's Supper he made the point that all those who took part in the Communion service should be ready to follow Christ all the way. He said that they should be willing to obey God and keep His commandments.

Pastor Wheeler's statement didn't set well with Mrs. Oakes, for as a Seventh Day Baptist she actually kept all the commandments of God, including the fourth—the command to keep holy the seventh day of the week. A woman of conviction, she spoke forcefully to the minister after the sermon, telling him quite plainly what she thought of his comment.

Wheeler's later testimony verified that the words "cut him to the quick." They sent him straight to his Bible to study the matter of Sabbathkeeping for himself. It was a turning point in his life. As he studied, he was convicted of the truth of the seventh-day Sabbath. He found that the fourth commandment is as binding now as when it was written in stone by God's own hand.

This incident occurred before the Great Disappointment of October 22, 1844, a time when few were aware of the seventh-day Sabbath. In 1840 Frederick Wheeler had been ordained as a minister in the Methodist Episcopal Church. He was a circuit-riding preacher, and Washington, New Hampshire, was one of his churches. He has the distinction of being the first ordained minister to preach in favor of the seventh-day Sabbath.

The Hillsboro Meeting

Although Hillsboro, Massachusetts, wasn't on a main thoroughfare, a camp meeting was scheduled to be held there in a grove owned by Washington Barnes, and Frederick Wheeler was excited to be a part of the meeting.

It took real interest on the part of the people just to make the effort to get there. In 1844 people were willing to undergo many inconveniences to hear the message of Jesus' soon coming, and this meeting at Hillsboro attracted between 300 and 400 people. They came by stage, wagon and carriage, and on horseback. It was even reported that a few people walked as far as 100 miles to attend the meetings. They brought their families, their food, and their makeshift tents. They were so happy to be there that they didn't mind the hardships.

Seats for the congregation were made by placing long tree trunks along the ground and putting rough boards across them. There was, of course, no organ or other musical instrument, but the singing was reported to have been extraordinarily beautiful.

Washington Barnes lived about two miles from the site. He was a well-to-do man who allowed the campers to turn their horses into his pastures. Not only that; he invited them to go over to his farm and take all the apples and potatoes they wanted. His wife and her sister, who was Mrs. Frederick Wheeler, didn't go to the meetings. Instead, they spent all their time baking bread for the campers. If a camper had money, he or she paid for the bread; if not, then it was free. A nearby farmer sold milk to those who needed it. It was a week that held many blessings for those who were looking for the Lord's soon appearing. It was a blessed week even for those women who spent their days in the kitchen, providing for the needs of the campers.

Planting a Garden

In anticipation of the return of Jesus, some of the Advent believers were sure it was a denial of faith to plant even a garden, let alone any field crops. After all, Jesus was coming soon, and there would be no need of crops. However, Mrs. Wheeler urged her husband to put in a garden; it was spring, and a garden would at least provide food for the summer.

But Elder Wheeler was so busy with his work of pastoring that he just didn't have time. One sunny day he came home to the surprise of his life. His wife had decided they could wait no longer to get the seeds in the ground, so she had taken matters into her own hands. She and their 10-year-old son had borrowed a plow and harnessed it to old Billy, the family horse. When Elder Wheeler came home, he found his wife and son planting the garden she'd been asking for. Of course, he couldn't stand to see his wife plowing, so he finished the chore himself. He found that he did have time after all.

Preaching the Gospel

Wheeler, along with other Advent believers, had put everything he had into spreading the good news. On October 23, the day after the Great Disappointment, he found himself "with less than a dollar, less than a peck of potatoes, not a whole suit of clothes, his shoes full of holes, with a wife and four children." Like many others, they endured sarcastic insults from their neighbors.

In order to make ends meet, Wheeler hired out as a farmhand, though he continued to preach as much as he could. Even though he had kept the seventh-day Sabbath for some time, on Sundays he rode half a day north to preach at a church in Claremont, New Hampshire. He received $4 a week that first year. But the next year he was in better financial shape, and he made no charge for the weekly trip.

In the summer of 1845 Wheeler and his wife did mission work among the people of Vermont. They left their four children and a cow with another of Mrs. Wheeler's sisters and her husband, Reuben Spalding. After about six weeks of teaching and preaching in Vermont, the Wheelers returned, gathered up their children and cow, and went home, both of them happy to have been of service to their Lord.

Mrs. Wheeler shared her husband's burden for the people, giving her time and energies to help with evangelistic work. She set a good example for the thousands of ministers' wives who followed her.

Wheeler's work had been largely limited to the general area of Washington, New Hampshire, but in 1851 James White suggested that he should go farther afield in his ministry. White reported in the *Review,* "We have been with [Elder Wheeler] in a number of meetings and are satisfied that he, with God's blessing, will exert a good influence and accomplish much in bringing out the hidden jewels of the Lord."

White urged the Washington church to support their man in the field and to be sure that his family was well cared for. On the strength of Elder White's urging, Wheeler held some evangelistic meetings in Connecticut. After a few meetings he sent home the message, "I'm firm in my faith in Christ and His return. I'll never lay down the armor. I'm here for the duration."

In 1852 he began expanding his work to other communities in New Hampshire and into Vermont. When Ellen White's brother Robert died of tuberculosis, Elder Wheeler happened to be near Gorham, Maine, and conducted the funeral service.

Henriette Kolb remembered Frederick Wheeler well: "I can still remember eagerly watching to see him come in sight, sitting up straight in his open buggy, drawn by Billy, his faithful old gray horse. We saw no ministers in those early days except on these occasions, and what a treat it was!"

Then in 1857, while attending a conference in Roosevelt, New York, Frederick Wheeler was asked to work in central New York. The churches in the area would "defray the expenses of removing his family to his field of labor, and support him in the field." That may be the first time the fledgling Adventist organization called a worker from one location to another and paid the moving expenses.

At one time Wheeler worked with S. W. Rhodes and Hiram Edson holding evangelistic meetings in New York. Finally retiring to a farm in West Monroe, New York, he reflected on his life: "I praise God that I have ever been permitted, not only to believe the truth, but to labor somewhat in connection with the work, and that through God's blessing on my feeble efforts some have been led to rejoice in the light and in hope of eternal life through Him."

At the age of 96 Frederick Wheeler sent a message to the New York camp meeting. It rang with the same sentiments he had written from his evangelistic trip to Connecticut: "The gospel armor I will not put off, the contest I will not yield, until with all the ransomed host I shout the final victory."

In 1902 Pastor Wheeler wrote a letter to his granddaughter in which he expressed his pleasure that she was getting a good education, and his hope that God would use her in His work. He also told her that for many years he had a very strong expectation that he would live to witness the "awfully sublime scenes connected with" the second coming of Jesus.

Then he went on to say, "But I shall likely fall asleep. I am not very anxious about it now, only that my days may close in peace so that I may share in the glorious rest that remains for the people of God. . . . I see also many mistakes and failures to regret. But I seek to confess all to the Lord and leave them with Him."

Frederick Wheeler lived a long life of loyal service to his God, ever faithful in following His leading and never faltering in his confidence. He died in 1910 at the age of 99 and is buried in West Monroe, New York. His works did follow him, and his tombstone proclaims that he was "a pioneer minister of Seventh-day Adventists."

Chapter 8

Anna Knight: Missionary to India and the South

Her errand completed, Anna decided that a bicycle ride through the park might help her relax a little before she went home. It had been a hot day, and the breeze felt cool as it blew against her warm face. Darkness was falling. Most people had gone home to dinner, and there was no one within her sight. That's when she heard the voice:

"Go home now. You've been out long enough. It's time to go home."

Looking around, she saw no one.

Oh, I must have imagined I heard a voice, she thought. *I'll just ride down the road to the bridge; then I'll go home.*

As she rode toward the bridge she thought how refreshing the breeze was after the heat of the day. At the bridge she turned around and started back the way she had come. A short distance ahead she noticed a man standing by the side of the road. Something told her to ride faster, but she thought this would just attract the man's attention. Again the voice came and in a commanding tone told her to ride faster.

She followed the instruction, her legs pumping as fast as she could. Closer and closer the man loomed in her vision. As she passed him, he jumped into the road and grabbed her bicycle from behind. She was going so fast that he couldn't stop her, but he did manage to turn her off the road, directly into the path of a large tree. In her mind's eye she could see her "brains splattered on the ground around the tree trunk." She just knew her time had come—she was going to die against that tree!

She barely had time to flash a prayer to God to save her. Instead of crashing into the tree, the front wheel smashed into the curb with such force that both the man and the bicycle came crashing down on top of her. She jumped quickly to her feet, yelling at the top of her lungs, "Police! Police! Help! Help!"

But no one was within hearing distance, and the man grabbed at her, trying to get his hands around her neck.

However, this petty thief hadn't reckoned with the self-reliant girl from Mississippi—or her God. She fought him tooth and nail. Each time his hands came near her neck, she was able to knock them away. Then his fingers caught in the cord that held her watch around her neck. The cord broke, and the watch fell to the ground. The robber scooped it up and disappeared into the park.

Anna felt sure her angel had tried to deliver her from the robbery. If she had obeyed the voice that told her to "go home," this nightmare never would have happened. The text in Exodus 23:20-22 came to her mind: "Behold, I send an Angel before thee, to keep thee in the way, and to bring thee into the place which I have prepared. Beware of him, and obey his voice. . . . If thou shalt indeed obey his voice . . . then I will be an enemy unto thine enemies, and an adversary unto thine adversaries."

It was a sadder and wiser young woman who reclaimed her bicycle and made her way home. What made her saddest of all was that her watch had been stolen.

The Watch

Earlier that day Anna Knight had been riding her bicycle rapidly through the crowded streets of Calcutta, India. She had skillfully maneuvered through the mass of humans, animals, and oxcarts as she made her way to the main post office. Her letter *had* to go out on the boat tomorrow.

Donna Humphrey, fellow missionary and friend, had died suddenly and unexpectedly. Anna grieved the loss of her teammate. Together they had come to India the year before, 1901. Close friends, they had worked well together as they traveled throughout India giving medical care and selling Christian books and magazines. Now in March 1902 Donna was gone.

Knowing that her relatives would be anxious to learn details of Donna's death, Anna pulled herself together and wrote, telling them everything she knew of the tragedy. This was the letter that needed to go on the boat the next day.

The watch that had been wrenched from her neck had been a gift from Donna. Now it was gone forever. She would never see either the gift or the giver again in this world. To her that was the most distressing part of the assault in the park.

An Appetite for Knowledge

Born into a poor Mississippi Black family in 1874, Anna Knight was a little girl with an enormous appetite for knowledge. Her mother, a freed slave, eked out a living by sharecropping. After several years she somehow saved enough money to buy 80 acres of land. The family managed to grow food for their own use, and they grew cotton as a cash crop. But the small amount of cash they received for the cotton was never enough to cover the needs of the large family. Anna grew up knowing what hard work was.

There were no schools for Black children, and Anna was not allowed to go to the school for Whites. Determined to learn all she could, she offered to help the White neighbor girls with their chores if they'd let her look at their books—and even teach her a little. They agreed, but they often neglected their promise to Anna so they could play. It was an uneven trade, but it was better than nothing.

Somewhere along the way, someone gave Anna an old Webster speller, which quickly became a cherished treasure. Then she got a *McGuffey's Reader,* and the two books became her prized possessions. On Sundays when the family went to visit relatives, the books went with her, for one of the favorite pastimes on visiting day was a spelling bee. Anna soon became skilled in reading and spelling. Before she ever went to school herself, she was teaching the younger children to read and do arithmetic.

Blessings From the "Exchange Column"

One bright sunny day a magazine came into Anna's possession, and she spotted an advertisement that was to change her life. The ad said that if the reader would send 10 cents, her name would be put on a list to receive free samples of books, papers, and catalogs. Oh, what treasure that would be! It took some time, but at last Anna managed to save 10 cents, and sent for the free samples. Before long they began to arrive in the Knight mailbox. Within one paper was an exchange column, through which readers could make requests for various items.

Using her best handwriting, Anna wrote to the column asking for some "nice reading material." Forty people answered her request. Two Seventh-day Adventists were among the 40. W. W. Eastman, a literature evangelist in Texas, sent her a big package of papers including the *Review and Herald, Youth's Instructor, Sabbath School Worker,* and *Medical Missionary.*

Edith Embree, in Oakland, California, sent her the *Signs of the Times* every week, and sometimes she even wrote a letter. She was employed at the Pacific Press, where *Signs of the Times* was published. She took Anna under her wing and taught her to love Jesus.

Anna devoured every word in every paper. She accepted the teachings she read, and soon became a Sabbathkeeper. Of course, that made life difficult, as there was nobody living near her who kept the Sabbath. Not unreasonably, her puzzled family objected to her "lying around all day on Saturday," while they still had to work. For this reason she often spent the day out in the woods so she could keep the Sabbath. She would take her Bible, *Sabbath School Worker,* Sabbath school quarterly, *Review and Herald,* and *Youth's Instructor* and spend the day in the great outdoors. If it rained, she'd go to the barn and spend the day in the hayloft. In the wintertime it was cozy there, and she enjoyed the sweet smell of the hay.

Spending Sabbath alone all day in the woods or in the hayloft could have been a very long day, but Anna enjoyed every moment of the Sabbath. She was never bored, for she spent the time memorizing the Sabbath school lesson and reading all the papers from cover to cover! She always took her dog with her, and he seemed to know that something special was happening on that day. Whenever a wild animal or a cow would come anywhere near, he would get up and quietly drive them away. He never barked at them on the Sabbath.

Though Anna Knight was still young, there were people who threatened her and said bad things about her because she was out of step with the rest of the community—she kept the seventh-day Sabbath. But she was faithful, and the Lord always protected her from those who bullied her.

Joining the Church

Edith Embree became Anna's mentor, teaching her about the Bible and the love of Jesus. She sent her the little book *Steps to Christ*, by Ellen G. White. Eagerly Anna read it and then reread it. It brought peace and happiness to her battered soul. She determined that she would be baptized into the church that printed that book and those wonderful papers Miss Embree sent her. She wrote to her friend, pouring out her heart's desire.

Knowing that some action was needed at once, Miss Embree wrote to the secretary of the Southern Missionary Tract Society, L. D. Chambers, who lived in Tennessee. She told him all about the Black girl in Mississippi who had come to know and love Jesus and wanted to be baptized into the Seventh-day Adventist Church. At that time there were no conferences in the South and not many organized churches. Graysville, Tennessee, was the closest church to Anna's home—382 miles away!

With the help of several individuals, arrangements were made for Anna to travel by train to Chattanooga, where she was met by Elder Chambers, who took her to his home in Graysville. After her baptism, it was planned that she would enroll in the school at Graysville for the current term of 10 weeks. What a thrill and a joy it was to Anna to be in a real school. We can imagine her excitement on the first day of school. How she woke up early and dressed with care. Her smile as she saw the building, went inside, and eagerly found a seat in the classroom.

The teachers and students were glad to have her, for she was bright and clever—and she was fun.

But word must have spread like wildfire: *a Black is enrolled in our school.* Some of the parents strongly objected to their children being in the same school with a Black. In a few short hours Anna's career at the Graysville school was over. She spent only one day as a student. She wasn't allowed to return.

The warmhearted superintendent of the school took the heartbroken girl into her own home. Anna helped with the housework, and the kind woman taught her until it was time for her to return to her own home. She had learned so much in those 10 weeks that none of her family ever had the slightest inkling that she didn't actually go to school. Although bitterly disappointed about not being allowed to attend classes, she never felt the need to tell her family about the crushing blow of not being accepted as a student.

After Anna was home again, life grew complicated because of her determination to keep the seventh-day Sabbath holy. She would not work in the fields on Sabbath, even when there was cotton to hoe or fields to plant. She *could* not. But her family—and community—did not understand. Then, too, she did not attend church with her family on Sunday. Her mother did not understand and took it as rebellion. At last both Anna and her family agreed that it probably would be better for her to leave home.

Life Changes

Again Anna made the long trip to Tennessee. She would live with Elder and Mrs. Chambers until they could find a way to send her to school. Elder Chambers met her at the Chattanooga station with a big surprise. It was a beautiful black cape, with a quilted satin lining that his wife had made for her. She had never owned such a beautiful article of clothing, and she cherished the cape and its memories for many years. Both Elder and Mrs. Chambers loved Anna and welcomed her into their home.

Mrs. Chambers was a milliner, a dressmaker, and a wonderful cook—the bread she made practically melted in the mouth. She had organized a group of women into a sort of club called the women's exchange, and they sold their baked goods and needlework at one of the big grocery stores in town. Anna worked for Mrs. Chambers, helping bake bread, as well as pies, cakes, and cookies. Some days they made 60 loaves of bread, and Anna carried them to the women's exchange as they came from the oven.

Mrs. Chambers was working extra hard to earn money for fabric to make clothing for Anna so she could go to school. As the motherly woman finished each dress, she would spread it across the bed and say: "Anna, I hope this will last you until the Lord comes." And Anna tried very hard to take good care of her clothes so they would last a long time, but in reality they didn't last very long.

One day as Anna was thinking of all that Elder and Mrs. Chambers were doing for her, she just couldn't keep from crying. She didn't want Mrs. Chambers to see her tears, so she went up to the attic to cry. When Mrs. Chambers found her there with the tears flowing down her cheeks, she was alarmed. She put her arms around the girl, asking: "My dear child, whatever is the matter? Have you had bad news from home?"

"Oh, no," sobbed Anna.

"Well, are you homesick? Do you want to see your mother?"

"No. I'm not homesick. I like living here."

"Well, then, have I hurt your feelings?"

"Oh, no, Mrs. Chambers, you could never hurt my feelings."

"Then, Anna, what in the world is the matter?"

"Oh, dear Mrs. Chambers, I've been thinking of all the nice things you do for me. I'm so poor, and I'll never be able to repay you for all your goodness and kindness to me!" And the tears fell thick and fast.

By that time Mrs. Chambers was shedding a few tears of her own, hugging Anna and reassuring her that she and her husband didn't expect or want pay for anything they did for her. They firmly believed that Anna would become a worker for God someday and that their work would go on through her.

Anna never forgot Mrs. Chambers' faith in her. Even when she was an old woman the memory of Mrs. Chambers' unselfish love stayed with her. Throughout her life it inspired her to go out of her way to help others.

Cooking for Camp Meeting

In 1894 Anna was enrolled in Mount Vernon Academy, in Ohio. When the school year ended, she went back to Elder and Mrs. Chambers in Graysville, Tennessee. At this time church officials had completed plans for a camp meeting to be held in Chattanooga. However, they hadn't yet found someone to take the responsibility of cooking for those who couldn't provide their own meals during the session. Because Anna lived with Elder and Mrs. Chambers and had attended Mount Vernon Academy, it was felt that she was well able to fulfill that obligation. They told her that about 40 people would need the cafeteria services.

Also in the area were two nurses from Battle Creek who had been sent to do self-supporting medical work in the South. They volunteered to help the young girl with the meals. Anna had been a church member for only about two years and had never even been to a camp meeting, much less cooked for one. She determined to do her best, but the facilities were practically nonexistent. For her use there was an old secondhand stove and a few kettles and pans borrowed from church members. In fact, just about everything was borrowed, and since there was no money for replacement, great care had to be taken that nothing be broken or lost.

The meeting became much larger than anyone expected, and the 40 meals three times a day became more like 100. For the first few days Anna was frightened and unsure of herself—there never seemed to be quite enough food, and while she was taking care of one pot of food another pot would boil over or scorch. The first Sabbath of camp meeting she served baked beans. The weather was very hot, and there was no icebox on the grounds. The beans didn't keep very well, and a few people got sick—just a little sick, not too bad—and, after all, there were two nurses there to take care of them!

Camp meeting lasted for 10 days, with six meetings each day. With all her duties, Anna was able to attend only six meetings during the entire 10 days. But the camp meeting itself was considered a great success and blessing. And for those who could attend the meetings, it was. As for Anna Knight, she was too busy fixing three meals a day for all the hungry people.

At the end of the camp meeting she was paid $5 for her work. She said she knew by experience the meaning of the verse "As thy days, so shall thy strength be." She never cooked for another camp meeting—and she never complained about the cooking at any other camp meeting she attended!

At Battle Creek

Elder Chambers arranged for Anna to enroll in the industrial school begun by the Paulson brothers in Battle Creek, Michigan. Arriving on campus, she left her letters of introduction with Dr. J. H. Kellogg and Prof. W. W. Prescott. She knew no one on campus. She had nothing in particular to do and no place to go while she waited to hear from the two men, so she decided to walk around the campus. Eventually she arrived at the laundry, where she found a girl she had known at Mount Vernon. This young woman and several others were ironing, so Anna picked up an iron and began ironing while she talked to them.

Unknown to Anna, there was a rule against unnecessary talking while working. The manager came along and, hearing the talk, stopped to ask Anna some questions—one of them being "Who sent you here?" Anna said she had nothing to do while she was waiting for her assignments and had stopped at the laundry. She was helping the other girls with their work. The manager smiled and left the room. Then the girls filled her in on the no-talking rule. No one was reprimanded, and she continued to iron.

When the campus jobs were assigned, Anna was given work at the laundry. The laundry supervisor wasn't very happy about having to take the two new girls who were "left over" after all the other jobs had been taken, but Anna determined to do her work well and quickly. As a result, the supervisor gave her praises and apologies, saying that she wished all the new workers were as efficient as Anna.

Anna was soon going to school four hours a day and working six hours. Then she was asked to take over the laundry "box room," which meant she would spend 10 hours a day at her job. All the women helpers and nurses had to come to the box room for their laundry. It wasn't long before Anna knew everyone, and she liked that. She also had some time to study while she was on duty. On the whole, it wasn't such a bad job assignment. It so happened that while on duty she was able to do some ironing for the nurses and medical students, and they paid her. She turned the money over to the supervisor, who gave it back to her, saying she should keep it for her needs. Anna worked in the laundry for almost a year, and the income enabled her to pay all her school expenses.

All this work didn't hurt her studies, either. During her year in the industrial, or preparatory, school she was able to earn the rest of the credits she needed to enroll in the nursing course. With what she was able to save from her earnings and some money sent to her by Elder and Mrs. Chambers, she was able to buy her schoolbooks when the next nursing class was formed.

Nurses' Training at Battle Creek College

One of the highlights of Anna's nurses' training came when Mrs. S.M.I. Henry was brought to Battle Creek Sanitarium as a patient. Dr. Kellogg himself was her attending physician, but he had to tell her that nothing short of a miracle could save her, for her heart was in serious trouble. Still Mrs. Henry decided to stay at the sanitarium for a time. One day as the chaplain visited with her she asked if she could be anointed, as outlined in James 5:14, 15. She said that she was a Christian, and all the doctors and helpers were Christians. Why then, she asked, couldn't she be healed?

A date was set for the anointing service. All who knew her were asked to pray, wherever they were, at the specified time. Mrs. Henry was helped into a wheelchair, and one of the doctors rolled her to the chapel. The service was quiet, sober, and spiritual. Though she'd been taken down the elevator in a wheelchair, *she walked back up the stairs* to her room. When the doctors examined her, there were no signs of the former heart disease. She had been healed.

Another outstanding event occurred during Anna's time at Battle Creek Sanitarium. The students were made aware of a serious famine in India, and that some of their own missionaries from the sanitarium faced a dire shortage of food. Dr. Kellogg called them all together—the doctors, nurses, students, and helpers—and appealed to them to make a sacrifice of their own food. They would go on a "Hindu diet" for one week, cutting out everything from their food bill except those things that the sanitarium didn't have to buy. (The sanitarium had big gardens and grew much of the food served there.)

More than 400 medical students, doctors, nurses, and helpers indicated that they were willing to go on the restricted diet. At the end of a week they had saved $500. They were so thrilled at the amount of money saved that they decided to continue the program for another week. As a result of their self-sacrifice, $1,000 was sent to India—all from the two-week savings on their food bill!

The missionaries were very thankful to those dedicated people in Battle Creek for the help they sent and for the lives that were saved as a result of their sacrifice. In fact, when Anna went to India as a missionary, she taught five of the orphan children whose lives had been saved by the help sent to the missionaries in Calcutta during the famine.

Nurse Knight Begins Self-supporting Work in Mississippi

After Anna graduated from Battle Creek Sanitarium's School of Nursing, Dr. Kellogg was very helpful in getting her started in self-supporting mission work in her home state of Mississippi. He made arrangements for her transportation back home and for her to get as many of his number one physiology books as she thought she would need for her work.

One of the first things she did when she got back to Ellisville, Mississippi, was to call a meeting of those who were interested in starting a school for their children. She showed them the books, charts, and the nurse's uniform that Dr. Kellogg had given her. She carefully explained that all her plans were for the good of their children and the whole community, and that she wanted them all to work together in letting the light of Christ come into their settlement.

It seemed that all the ill feelings against Anna in previous years had disappeared. The people were glad to have her back in their midst, eager to make life better for all of them. The first year the only building they could find for their school was an old log cabin on the farm of Anna's uncle. It was run-down and falling down, but it had a pretty good roof and a fireplace that worked. So people got busy. Two benches were made from logs, each bench long enough to seat about nine children. In addition, a homemade chair and table were provided for the teacher.

Anna's pay for teaching this school was a dollar a week—paid in a combination of cash and labor. Both parents and children participated in the plan. The children were given a credit of five cents an hour to cut wood for the school fireplace, and this helped them feel they were paying something toward their schooling.

At the close of the school year Dr. Kellogg asked Anna and a few others who had gone out to do pioneer missionary work to come back to Battle Creek. They could take a postgraduate course as well as help care for the large number of patients who came to the sanitarium during the summer. Anna accepted the offer. She was able to attend summer school part of the time, and received training that helped her with her mission school in Mississippi.

A New Schoolhouse

Anna established a building fund so the community could have a new schoolhouse to replace the old tumbledown cabin. She planted four acres of cotton that the women and children of the community picked. The cotton was then sold and the money put into the building fund. Though the estimates for the simple building were high, Anna knew they could raise the money. In about eight weeks the building was completed. It was a real community effort, and most of the citizens were proud to have such a nice school for their children.

That year there were 24 students in eight grades, and tuition was a dollar a month. Only one family was able to pay the tuition in cash. The rest paid in cash and labor.

Part of Anna's plan was to hold two school sessions each Sunday. The meeting places were about six miles apart. After the Sunday sessions were over, she then held some basic reading, writing, and arithmetic lessons for the adults who wanted to attend. She also taught them better ways of health and temperance.

Trouble From the Moonshiners

The making and selling of illegal whiskey was a thriving business in some parts of the South, and moonshiners in the area didn't appreciate in the least what Anna was teaching the people about the effects of whiskey on their hearts, livers, and other organs. They sent word to Anna to stop preaching against their business or they'd put *her* out of business. Her word to them was that she wasn't preaching, only teaching. But if they were ready to shoot, she was ready too. Her friends were upset about all of this, but she wasn't worried. She had faith that God was guiding her. However, to make her friends feel better about her safety she carried a revolver and sometimes a double-barreled shotgun, both of which she was well able to use.

One afternoon as she was returning home from one of her Sunday school sessions, Anna saw in the distance several of the men who had threatened her. They had come into a lane that was fenced on both sides, so she couldn't just turn another way and get away from them.

She was riding a horse that she had trained some years before, one who knew her well and responded to her signals. She rode on as though she suspected nothing amiss until she got fairly near the men. Then she dropped the reins, threw up her hands, and slapped the horse on his sides. This was the signal for him to run as fast as he could—and he took off! She leaned over as though trying to catch the reins, but she was actually urging him to go faster. The startled mob fired their guns, but neither the horse nor Anna was harmed. Long moments later, safely away from danger, Anna gently patted the horse, and he stopped running. She and the horse arrived safely at their destination.

Within a few hours it was time for her second Sunday session of school. The class had barely begun when three of these same men came into the schoolhouse and took a back seat. They had been drinking. Soon one of them spat on the floor. Anna had a no-spitting-on-the-floor rule. She stopped in midsentence and looked straight at the man, saying, "I thought I heard someone spit on the floor. If so, please don't do it again. If I'm not correct, I beg your pardon." This courteous attitude was unexpected, and the men looked at each other, then got up and walked out.

Anna continued teaching, though she watched and listened for the intruders' next move. When she saw that they had gone into the woods instead of going to the road, she knew the confrontation wasn't over. She sent the women and children home, closed up the schoolhouse, and went to her own home. Two of the men in her family stayed behind to see what would happen next. A short time later the three men reappeared at the schoolhouse even drunker than they had been before. The five men were soon in a fierce fistfight. The troublemakers quickly found that the two Knights were too much for the three of them, and they gave up and left.

Anna didn't close her school just because of a little trouble. She had watchmen guard the building at night, and every day she took her guns as well as her books to school. Her work went on. When the evil men saw she wasn't afraid, they made no more trouble.

Service in India

Knowing of Anna's successful work in Mississippi, Dr. John Harvey Kellogg invited her to attend the 1901 General Conference session at Battle Creek.

While she was there she felt God calling her to serve Him in another mission field. After arranging for friends to carry on her work in Mississippi, she answered God's call to serve Him in India. She stayed there six years, ministering to the needs of the people. She served as both a nurse and a literature evangelist, selling books and papers such as the *Oriental Watchman*. The Lord protected her as she sometimes traveled in dangerous parts of the country by train, oxcart, and bicycle. He also blessed her abundantly as she sought and followed His leading in even the smallest detail. Because of Anna Knight many people in India came to know the God of heaven and commit their lives to Him.

On Furlough

At the end of her six-year term Anna came home on furlough, intending to return to India in two years. During those two years in the States she planned to establish another school among her own neighbors in the South. The school she had built near her home in Ellisville, Mississippi, had been burned, and she wrote to the people there asking them to build another school, this time near the center of town. Every minute of her two-year furlough counted, so she wanted to begin school as soon as possible. At the first meeting held in the new schoolhouse the entire community turned out to welcome her. Even some of the men who had burned the other school were there. Everyone seemed glad to see her and to hear the stories of her work in India.

As she spoke to the people that day she reminded them that back in 1898, when she had established a school, none of them could read or write.

She reassured them that there were better days ahead for them and their children, but there wouldn't be time for parties, dances, and other questionable forms of amusement. She asked for a show of commitment from her former students and others who were interested enough to follow her plan for a better way of life. The next Monday morning 22 children and young people were at the school, ready to take up their studies. Anna taught long hours and resumed her Sunday school sessions as well. She also gave Bible studies in many of the surrounding communities. Within six months nine people were ready for baptism, among them Anna's mother and two of her sisters.

A New Mission Field

The Southeastern Union was eager to establish a medical work for Black people in the South, and in 1909 Anna was asked to help open a sanitarium in Atlanta, Georgia. She made it a subject of prayer, earnestly seeking to know the Lord's will. The result was that instead of going back to India, she went to a new mission field in the South. Unfortunately, the idea of a sanitarium for Black people in that neighborhood of Atlanta didn't set well with the community, and the mayor denied the permit. A treatment room was opened instead. After a slow start it became a success and was a real help to poor people in that area.

Anna's experience and work in India made her a sought-after speaker for commencement exercises at the four Black colleges in Atlanta. This led to other speaking invitations, and as she made friends, the prejudice against Blacks and Seventh-day Adventists lessened somewhat.

A School in Atlanta

About 1911 Anna was asked to help with the two-teacher mission school being operated in Atlanta. As more students applied to the school it became necessary to hold night classes for the older pupils. The demand was so high that there wasn't room for all who wanted to attend. The school must be enlarged, but there was no money to finance such an ambitious plan. They needed more desks and a bigger stove to serve the larger room. They were in uncharted waters. It was a new endeavor in the South, and no one really knew how to go about financing or executing a plan for expansion.

Anna had been appointed chair of the school board. If the expansion was to happen, it was up to her to find the money. First she went to the Southeastern Union Conference to see if they could help. Unfortunately, they couldn't. This was a mission school, and the conference already was paying 50 percent of the teachers' salaries. They couldn't see their way clear to finance anything else. She then broached the subject of buying the stove and desks on an installment plan. This was most unusual at that time, but the officials gave their approval.

For the previous eight years Anna had been in India and Mississippi. It didn't get so cold in those climates, but winters in Atlanta were very cold. As she didn't have a much-needed coat, Anna had been saving a little money here and there so she could buy one before winter. But without hesitation she took her coat money and went to the hardware store, where she made a down payment on a stove that would fit the needs of the school. She promised to make small monthly payments until it was paid for.

Her next stop was the school supply house, where she presented her need and her payment plan. The managers there talked it over and agreed to sell her the desks and let her pay a small amount each month until they were paid for. The next day the stove and the desks were delivered and set up.

Shouts of joy rang out as the students feasted their eyes on the shiny new desks set in orderly rows across the room. The polished black stove that gave out such warmth was a delight to one and all. But it wasn't paid for. What would happen if the pupils failed to pay their tuition? Anna discussed the matter with the school board, reminding them that the Lord who had opened the way for the school to be enlarged could impress the patrons that they could and should pay their tuition. God honored their faith, and the fees were paid. The school was a great success.

However, Anna's coat money was gone. Winter was almost upon them, and she knew she wouldn't be able to save enough to get a coat that year. While she was willing to buy on credit the necessary desks and a stove for the school, she would go without a coat rather than buy one on credit for herself.

God Provides at Coat for Anna

A few days later she responded to a letter from her old friend Miss

Embree, who was now Mrs. Runnels. Anna wrote about her work in Atlanta, the school, and how she had spent her little bit of savings on desks and a stove. She told Mrs. Runnels that the work of God must come first and that she was glad she had the few dollars set aside so it could be used in this emergency.

Mrs. Runnels shared the letter with her group of Missionary Volunteers in California, and they suggested that they take up an offering to replace the coat money. A friend who had known Anna in Battle Creek happened to be at the meeting. She'd been given a coat to pass on to someone in need, and she was sure the coat would fit Anna perfectly. She would ship it by express mail the next day.

The package arrived that very week, and Anna opened it excitedly. Inside she found a lovely black coat, almost new—and a perfect fit. Furthermore, it was of better quality than she would have bought for herself. But there was more. In addition to the coat, the Missionary Volunteers had sent money—enough to pay off the remaining debt on the stove. From that time onward Philippians 4:19 was one of Anna's favorite texts: "But my God shall supply all your needs according to his riches in glory by Christ Jesus."

Traveling, Traveling

At the time Anna Knight was baptized into the Seventh-day Adventist Church, the work in the South was scattered and unorganized. What is known now as the Southern Union Conference was a mission field, and there were only 50 Black Seventh-day Adventists throughout North America. No wonder she had to travel 382 miles to be baptized!

By 1909, when Anna began the health work in Atlanta, Georgia, the Southeastern Union Conference had been organized. It had been formed from a part of the territory belonging to the Southern Union Conference. The work of the Seventh-day Adventist Church in the South was becoming a well-established entity.

Anna spent about six years pioneering the educational work for Blacks in the South, working first in the Southeastern Union Conference. She planned her work a month in advance, completing her itinerary in one conference before moving on to the next. She tried to visit all the church schools twice a year. When she transferred to the Southern Union, she was offered an office at union headquarters, but refused it. "No," she said. "My work is in the field with the schools and churches. I have no time or need for an office."

She traveled so much that it seemed she lived almost exclusively on the train. She tried to give her reports to the union office in person, but if that wasn't possible, she always sent a detailed written report. Meanwhile, she had moved her permanent residence to Oakwood College, in Huntsville, Alabama.

About 1916 Anna was called back to the Southeastern Union Conference. She didn't feel much inclined to accept the invitation, but she prayed about it and was impressed by the Lord to accept the change. She made several conditions to her acceptance, one of them being that she be permitted to continue living at Oakwood. The president was happy to agree, but urged her to begin her new work immediately.

The work she'd previously done in the Southeastern Conference hadn't made much progress, for there had been no real supervision. It took about six months of hard work to get everything reorganized and functioning. The teachers all across the union were happy to see her back, and she was heartily welcomed at all the schools and churches.

The Southern and Southeastern union conferences were once again combined to form the new Southern Union. At that time, 1932, Anna was elected as associate secretary of the Education, Home Missionary, Missionary Volunteer, and Sabbath school departments of the new Southern Union Conference Colored Department. She was reelected to this position at each union session until December 1945, when regional conferences were formed. A year later she formally retired.

An Honored Pioneer

During the last year of her life, when she was 98 years old, she served as president of the National Colored Teachers' Association. That also was the year that Anna was given the General Conference Department of Education's Medallion of Merit Award. At that time only 12 such awards had ever been made.

Anna Knight is a pioneer to remember. She spent her life "living by principle." She would pray, then continue to work until God made clear what the next move should be.

Her carefully kept records show that she conducted 9,388 meetings, made 11,744 missionary visits, wrote 48,918 letters, and traveled the equivalent of 23 trips around the world—not including her trips to, from, and within India. The chronicle of her travels and the details of the enormous amount of work she did leave a rich history of her work.

The fruit of Anna Knight's life proved that one committed, consecrated Christian can make a difference in the world in which he or she lives. Anna Knight was young when she caught God's vision of service, and she was willing to use the talents He gave her for the good of others. There's no doubt that her works do follow her.

Vignettes

Little Anna stood looking at the most beautiful objects she had ever seen. More than anything in the world she longed to possess them. To anyone else they might not have rated a second glance, but to a child who had so little pleasure and beauty in her life they were magnificent.

The salesman had made a routine call at the Knights' humble home. He was selling subscriptions for a magazine called *The Home and Fireside Magazine*. Best of all, he was giving a premium with each order: two large prints of George and Martha Washington and several smaller prints—all for $1.

Anna's mother did happen to have a dollar that day, but she certainly didn't intend to use it for such foolishness. She couldn't read; what did she need with a magazine?

But Anna could read, and she desperately wanted that magazine and those pictures. She begged and pleaded, and made such a fuss that Mrs. Knight grew embarrassed and finally relented. Once the salesman had departed, she had a few choice words for her daughter. Anna clearly understood that if she ever caused such a scene again, she would be eating her meals off the mantel for a week—if they had a mantel!

When the coveted materials arrived, Mother enjoyed looking at them and hearing Anna read from the magazine. When there was writing in script in the magazine, Anna would take it outside and practice writing in the sand until she mastered a beautiful handwriting.

Sometimes the children were allowed to go swimming in the creek. The men and women went on alternate days—never together on the same day. On one memorable day Anna and the other children ran on ahead of their mothers. They had been cautioned to stay near the shore, as farther out there was quicksand and also what was known as a suckhole. But for some unknown reason Anna went out too far. Suddenly her feet touched the quicksand, and the current swept her off her feet, carrying her directly toward the suckhole.

"Hurry, Hurry! Come quick!" the children yelled to Anna's mother. "Anna's drowning! Anna's drowning!"

Thinking quickly, Mrs. Knight jumped into the water slightly downstream from her daughter. As Anna was hurled along, the water swept her close enough for her mother to catch her with one hand and give her a mighty shove toward the shore. Mrs. Knight was then able to swim to her and pull her up onto dry ground. After Anna was revived and her mother was sure she was all right, she was severely scolded for her disobedience. Her carelessness could easily have ended in tragedy.

On the heels of her lecture on obedience, Mrs. Knight told Anna that she must learn to swim. She couldn't go through life afraid of the water. Mother would teach her to swim.

In later years Anna said she finally learned to swim. But she'd always add that the greatest lesson she learned was that "the way of the transgressor is hard" and "to obey is better than sacrifice." It was a hard lesson, but she learned not to take unnecessary risks and to obey those who were older and wiser than she.

On Sundays—the only real leisure time they had—Anna often would gather the younger children together and play school. When they tired of that, they would practice throwing rocks. They would each pick up small stones and take turns throwing them at a tree to see how many times they could hit the target. Of course Anna kept a careful record, and the one who got the most hits won the game.

The stone throwing proved to be quite practical in their daily life, and they all became experts in driving the hogs and cattle away from their fields.

Chapter 9

Nathaniel D. Faulkhead: Secret Societies

With Nathaniel D. Faulkhead's reputation as a businessman of unusual ability, it wasn't long after he and his family had accepted the Advent message (in about 1886 or 1887) that he was named treasurer of the Echo Publishing House in Australia. He worked hard, mastered the job, and produced good results.

Nathaniel Faulkhead was a prominent member not only of the Masons but of several other secret societies. His ambition was to reach the highest office in the Masons, and when he accepted the Adventist teachings he saw no reason to resign from the secret organizations to which he belonged. However, as the months passed and he became more and more involved in his lodge activities, he began to lose interest in the work of God. His fellow publishing house workers could see his increasing fascination with the secret societies and were concerned about his spiritual well-being.

Soon after her arrival in Australia in 1891, Mrs. White was given a detailed vision of conditions in the Echo Publishing House. She wrote out the entire vision, including personal testimonies to several of the individuals concerned. One of the testimonies was addressed to N. D. Faulkhead and his wife.

The entire written testimony came to 50 pages. At first she planned to mail it to Mr. Faulkhead, but a voice seemed to say, "No, this isn't the right time. Don't send it yet. They won't accept it now."

Twelve months later the testimony still hadn't been sent to the Faulkheads. The time still wasn't right.

In December 1892 J. H. Stockton, a fellow worker, was trying to talk to Nathaniel about his relationship with the Lord. He asked him a forthright question: "Brother Faulkhead, what would you do if Sister White had a testimony for you?"

"Well," was the curt reply, "it would have to be pretty strong for me to believe it was from God."

At that point neither Faulkhead nor Stockton was aware that God had shown the whole situation to Ellen White a year earlier.

Not long after this conversation Nathaniel dreamed that the Lord had given Ellen White a message for him. This dream, together with his rather testy response to Mr. Stockton, caused him to do some serious thinking.

Closing exercises of the first term of the Australasian Bible School were held about the middle of December 1892. Mrs. White had been in Ballarat, but on Monday, December 12, she returned to Melbourne in time for the special event, happily participating in the morning's program. Taking advantage of the fact that a number of the school board members were in town, W. C. White called a meeting of the board. N. D. Faulkhead, treasurer of the Echo Publishing House, was one of the members.

Mr. Faulkhead had been thinking of his dream that Ellen White had a message for him, and after the board meeting he went to see her. She was resting, but welcomed him with a pleasant greeting. He came right to the point, asking if she had a message for him. She suggested that he arrange a time to come back with his wife, and she would talk with them both. But he eagerly inquired, "Oh, Sister White, can't you give me the message now?"

In spite of her fatigue from the long trip and the activities of the morning, she agreed to talk to him. She shared with him the fact that several times she had been at the point of sending him the message by mail, but she "had felt forbidden by the Spirit of the Lord to do so." He hadn't been ready to receive it.

Apparently now he was ready, and she spent some time going over the part of the 50-page testimony dealing with work at the publishing house. Then she moved on to the personal testimony for Mr. Faulkhead. If he expected a glowing word of thanks from the Lord for the good work he was doing, he was doomed to disappointment.

As she talked to him and read from the manuscript, Mrs. White used gestures and words known only to members of the lodges. Nathaniel hardly knew how to relate to this phenomenon, and interrupted to ask if she knew what she'd done. She wasn't aware that she'd done anything unusual. Excited but puzzled, he told her that she had made a secret sign known only to Masons. As they talked on, she made another sign, which she later said was a sign her attending angel made to her.

Faulkhead turned pale. This sign was known only to the highest order of Masons. In fact, he had learned it just a few days earlier, and it was known only to six people in all of Australia. No woman could possibly know this sign.

This convinced Nathaniel that the testimony was from God. The Holy Spirit was working mightily for him. When she made another sign and he again interrupted, Ellen White was happily surprised, for she wasn't aware of having made any unusual movements. Nathaniel immediately thought of his recent words to Mr. Stockton about how a message would have to be *mighty strong* for him to believe it was from the Lord. This was strong stuff!

Knowing that his mother wasn't well, Willie White felt that the interview had gone on far too long, and he finally sent May Walling into the room to terminate the discussion. But May was sent away. Willie wondered what in the world was going on, but he knew his mother well enough to know that something vitally important was happening.

More time went by, and Willie felt he surely must bring the interview to a close. This was taking far too much of his mother's time and energy. He knocked on her door and called to her, but she sent him away also. There was a soul at stake, and she was fighting for God's possession of it. She continued her talk with Mr. Faulkhead.

Finally, after more than three hours, God and His angels prevailed, and Nathaniel Faulkhead surrendered everything to God. He told Mrs. White he would no longer be connected with the Masonic order or any of the other secret organizations to which he belonged. He said it would take him about nine months to wind up his business with them and sever connections with the three lodges under his direct control. His response to the Lord's message was "I accept every word. All of it belongs to me. . . . I accept the light the Lord has sent me through you. I'll act upon it. . . . I'll attend no more of their meetings, and shall close my business relations with them as fast as possible."

"Sister White," he said, "I wish you to know how I look upon this matter. I regard myself as greatly honored of the Lord. He has seen fit to mention me, and I'm not discouraged but encouraged. I shall follow out the light given me of the Lord."

True to his word, he sent in his resignation to the secret societies, and though he was pressured to continue his positions with them, he stood by his commitment to God. He found it to be a greater struggle than anticipated, but he stood firm, and the Lord blessed him abundantly.

Nathaniel Faulkhead became a strong, positive influence in the work of God because he was willing to accept the counsel of the Lord.

CHAPTER 10

Stephen Nelson Haskell: "Man of Action"

A few days before he died, Mr. How—the owner of a nice farm—called 17-year-old Stephen Haskell to his bedside. He explained that he knew he didn't have long to live and that he needed help. Under the circumstances it was likely that Stephen responded by saying:

"Of course, Mr. How. If there's anything I can do for you, just tell me."

But he certainly wasn't prepared for what followed.

Mr. How was leaving his farm and everything on it for young Haskell to manage. He knew Stephen well enough to trust him with all he had—including his invalid daughter, Mary.

"Stephen," he said, "I'm asking you to look after Mary. You know that I've been both father and mother to her. She's unable to take care of herself, and I don't know what to do. It's a lot to ask of a young man, but, Stephen, would you look after her? She has no one else in all the world."

Stephen gulped; he was only 17. He was a hired hand. And Mr. How was asking him to take care of his partially paralyzed daughter! How could he possibly do such a thing? True, he had helped Mr. How when Mary needed to be carried in and out of the house or from room to room. And true, he was fond of her. But was he mature enough and wise enough to be entirely responsible for her?

Asking for a little time to think it over, he finally decided, "All right, Mr. How, I'll do my best not only to take care of the farm, but to take care of Mary as well."

It was not a decision Stephen took lightly. He had helped Mr. How on the farm for perhaps a year or so and knew the routine of the work. However, taking care of Mary was another matter entirely.

In the days before and immediately after Mr. How's death, Stephen thought long and hard about how he would fulfill his promise to take care of Mary. The only appropriate way he could think of was to marry her. He wasn't quite 18, and she was 40! But he'd promised to take care of her. Not knowing how else to keep his word, he talked it over with her, and she accepted his proposal, saying that she did love him.

Young Stephen

Stephen Haskell was born in Oakham, Massachusetts, on April 22, 1833—the year the stars fell. At an early age he exhibited calm composure and good reasoning powers. He quickly made good decisions and stood by them. He was converted at the age of 15 and joined the Congregational Church. However, both Stephen and Mary were Methodists when they married, and their faith served to strengthen each other as they prayed that her health would improve. Within a couple of years her health was so much better that she was able to resume most of her former activities. It was said that Mary How Haskell could "manage spirited horses as few men could." Haskell writes that they always kept one to three horses.

Stephen's work for the Lord was never compromised by this May-December marriage. Before she'd become ill, Mary had been a teacher. She had good taste, and she enjoyed writing poetry. More than that, she encouraged him in his quest for education. There is no doubt that they enjoyed reading together from the large library she had acquired.

Come and Preach to Us

Mary and Stephen had been married a little more than two years when he heard the message that Christ was coming back to earth very soon. The sermon he heard thrilled him, and even though he was only 19 years old he began to share the good news with everybody he came in contact with. The "blessed hope"—he always called it—was his favorite topic of conversation.

One day as he talked enthusiastically with a friend, he began to turn from scripture to scripture to prove his points. His friend said to him,

"Stephen, why don't you preach? You ought to rent a hall and preach."

"Well, maybe I will" was the half-joking response. "If you'll rent the hall, I'll preach."

His friend hadn't been joking, and it wasn't long before he came knocking on the Haskell door. "We've got the hall," he said. "Now come and preach to us."

What! Him preach? This was more than young Haskell had bargained for. But he couldn't back out now. A date and time were set, and he repeated, almost verbatim, the only sermon he had heard on the subject of Jesus' second advent.

His listeners eagerly gathered around him afterward, asking for more studies. A small group was formed, and they began to study the Scriptures together. Stephen Haskell was filled with the love of Jesus and shared it with all those he met. It seemed that in his mind he kept hearing the words *You need to preach! You need to preach!* He didn't know whether this was his own desire or whether God was speaking to him.

He also had Mary to consider—after all, he had a wife to support. He was a professional soapmaker, selling his own product on a regular sales route around the country. This, of course, often took him away from home for weeks at a time. As he traveled by horse and buggy, he sometimes let the horse mosey along while he worked algebra problems, eventually conquering the subject. Following the logic he found in solving algebra problems, he made points in his sermons that were firm and sound, based not on algebra but on the formula of comparing scripture with scripture, thus reaching correct conclusions from the Word of God. It may well have been Mary who suggested that the mastery of algebra would strengthen the logical thinking needed to make his sermons powerful and emphatic.

Preaching in Canada

Stephen had business in the little town of Lake Consecon, Ontario, Canada—probably selling his soap. At one place, when his business call was finished, he spoke to the woman about the soon coming of Jesus. She promptly invited him to hold a meeting in her home that very evening. Word was sent around the community, and a large group of eager listeners gathered to hear Stephen Haskell explain the Word.

He saw this as the ideal opportunity to put himself to the test. If he failed there, where no one knew him well, it wouldn't be quite so embarrassing as it would be where he was well known. However, if his preaching brought conversion and baptism to even one person, he would see that as a signal that God was calling him to the ministry.

After the meeting the woman told Stephen that she had dreamed about him the night before, and when he knocked on her door that day she recognized him. In the dream she had noticed how he was dressed. His trousers were of a strange color and much too short for him—just as she had seen in the dream. Because of the dream she had felt impressed to invite him to hold a meeting in her home. She was so sure that Stephen had a message for the people of her community that it was decided to hold more meetings in a larger place—a schoolhouse not far away, where more people could be accommodated.

After preaching in the schoolhouse for about 10 days, he was invited to another area. In spite of the good attendance, Haskell still wasn't sure it was God's voice calling him, for there had been no baptism.

As he started his four-mile walk to the second appointment, a man came along and offered him a ride in his wagon. He told Haskell that he and his wife had been attending the meetings, and they both had been converted and wanted to be baptized. When Stephen visited them a few days later, he found 25 more people asking for baptism! His heart sang. This was the sign he had asked for. He would devote his life to preaching.

Of course, young Mr. Haskell wasn't an ordained minister, but he went right ahead and baptized each candidate. One older man threatened Haskell that if he tried to baptize his wife, he would wade right into the water and take her away by force. Reassuring the man's wife that the Lord had given instructions to "believe, and be baptized," and that God Himself would take care of any problems her husband might cause, Stephen went on with the baptism.

As the husband watched from the edge of the lake, the Holy Spirit came upon him with such power that right there he gave his own heart to Jesus and asked Stephen to baptize him as well.

Thus began Stephen Haskell's preaching career.

The Seventh-day Sabbath

In 1853 young Haskell attended a camp meeting held by the Advent believers in Winsted, Connecticut. Two or three other aspiring young preachers were with him. Before going home, he decided to take a little detour to Canada and visit the Adventist group that had been formed as a result of his visit the previous year.

Arriving at the Springfield, Massachusetts, train station, Stephen didn't quite know what to do with his trunk. He wanted to leave it somewhere and pick it up on his return from Canada. William Saxby, a Sabbathkeeper who was a tinsmith for the railroad, offered to store the trunk in his shop as long as necessary. Stephen gratefully accepted the offer. Then he and Saxby joined the other men as they talked about their plans for the evening.

The conversation turned to the Sabbath question. Haskell listened intently, but he heard nothing that validated observance of the seventh day. When Mr. Saxby began to talk to him, he curtly replied, "If you want to keep that old Jewish Sabbath, you can do so, but I never shall."

William Saxby apparently was a good judge of character, and he had a hunch that this young fellow was an honest man. Inviting Stephen to his home for supper, Mr. Saxby spoke of some of the truths he had been learning, such as the sanctuary and the soon coming of Jesus—but he didn't say a word about the Sabbath.

Haskell didn't believe all that Saxby said, but he did determine that he would study carefully and find out about these things for himself. He would be well prepared for the next fanatic who tried to sidetrack him with some off-the-wall teaching. When he left the Saxby home, he was given some small tracts, one of which was "Elihu on the Sabbath."

After leaving Springfield, Haskell traveled by boat toward a location known as the "Carrying Place." The small community was at the head of Consecon Lake, in Canada, and he planned to hold meetings there. As the boat moved smoothly along on the water, Haskell read and reread the Sabbath tract. There was nothing but Scripture there, and he couldn't argue with that. He kept thinking about all the things Mr. Saxby had told him. When the boat made a stop at Trent, about five miles from his destination, Haskell got off and went alone into the woods to settle this Sabbath question for himself.

He spent the day reading his Bible and praying about the Sabbath. Just before dark he came to the conclusion that, according to everything he had been studying, the seventh day was indeed the Sabbath. He had to admit that William Saxby had taught the truth and that Stephen Haskell must accept it. At that, he canceled the rest of his trip and returned home to begin preaching the newfound truth of the Sabbath.

He didn't go into preaching full-time, however. He had discovered that there wasn't much money in preaching, unless the audience was unusually generous. He and Mary still lived on their farm, and he kept up his soapmaking business. In this way he managed to make a living and still fill his heart's desire to preach the gospel message.

Soon Stephen had a group keeping the seventh-day Sabbath. The next summer he attended an Adventist meeting at Worcester, Massachusetts, hoping that he would be able to present the Sabbath question to the people in attendance. He was disappointed when he didn't have even one opportunity to preach during the session.

However, he met Thomas Hale, who invited him to his home in Hubbardston. As a result he and Mary rented rooms in the Hale home for the winter. There was a small group of Adventists in the town, and they were more than happy to have young Mr. Haskell preach to them every Sunday. The Hales and others soon accepted the seventh-day Sabbath, and meetings were held on Sabbaths, Sundays, and two evenings each week.

Only a few months earlier Mary Haskell had met William Saxby and heard him present the Sabbath question in such a way that she had been convicted of its importance. The Haskells and the Saxbys became good friends, often visiting in each other's homes.

Joseph Bates Comes to Teach

One cold winter day Haskell answered a knock at the door of the Hale home. A friendly middle-aged man introduced himself as an Adventist preacher who observed the seventh-day Sabbath. Their mutual friend, William Saxby, had asked him to call on them. "William," he said, "wrote and asked me to spend a little time with you, instructing you more fully in Bible truth."

Joseph Bates was welcomed into the home, and they were soon immersed in Bible study. Bates also preached to the members of the little group in Hubbardston. The Hales and others found these teachings of interest, and a Bible study group was formed, meeting around the long table in the Hales' kitchen. Bates stayed about 10 days in Hubbardston, tracing the lines of Bible prophecy, the earth's history, and the great controversy between good and evil. He spent even more time on his favorite topic—the three angels' messages of Revelation 14.

Bates outlined the important doctrines of salvation, turning from text to text as his students eagerly followed. They readily accepted the new light as their minds were opened.

Haskell later wrote, "He preached to us from breakfast till noon, and from dinner till night, and in the evening we had a general meeting. At that time I subscribed for the *Review* and have taken it ever since."

The Haskells also ordered a copy of each tract and paper published by the Review and Herald. A new and enthusiastic leader was born.

Life in South Lancaster

Leaving Hubbardston and settling at South Lancaster, Massachusetts, in 1864, Stephen and Mary bought property known as the Bancroft house, along with another piece of land nearby. At the rear of the property was a large building used as a carriage house and sometimes as a wagon repair shop. Haskell moved the building to another lot, where it served as a church for the Adventists who were quickly growing in number. As new Adventist families moved to South Lancaster, church membership soon became so large that a more adequate meeting place became necessary.

Haskell was not even licensed to preach, but he was so interested in the growing flock in South Lancaster and the surrounding towns that when he heard of a need, he was there to meet it. Sometimes his business customers expressed an interest in Bible truth, and he was more than happy to take time to teach them.

Stephen Haskell knew nothing about Adventist organization. He did realize there should be some way of reporting activities in his work, so on his own initiative he created a report form, giving the number of Sabbath schools and churches in New England, along with membership numbers and other items.

James and Ellen White were in South Lancaster in 1868 to attend a meeting, and Haskell handed his report to Elder White, who looked at it, smiled, and passed it along to J. H. Waggoner and J. N. Andrews.

The three men were well impressed by Haskell's abilities. They met as a committee and brought in a recommendation that Massachusetts, New

Hampshire, Rhode Island, and Connecticut be organized into a conference, and that Stephen N. Haskell be ordained to the ministry and be made the president of the new conference.

Of this Haskell said: "I wouldn't have been more surprised if I had been nominated as president of the United States."

The new conference wasn't actually formed until 1870, but Haskell took up his leadership duties in an unofficial way. He seemed to be "the right leader for a difficult field like the Northeast." He was described as having a "kind, ruddy face, neatly combed hair, and an ample beard." He was only 37 when he became conference president. The people had great confidence in him.

Since he was such a sociable, outgoing man, with a quick, winning smile, he made friends easily. He was always ready to talk to anyone. That's probably why he was so successful in his soapmaking enterprise. He was friendly and outgoing—and he had a good product that he liked to talk about. By the same token, he was always ready to talk about Jesus and His love for His children.

The Vigilant Missionary Society

Four women in the church at South Lancaster felt such a burden for their children that they met together in a prayer band. Others joined them, and they began meeting once a week to pray and share their experiences. This led them to write letters of encouragement to others. They also began visiting their neighbors, lending them books and papers, praying with and for them, and sharing with them their hope of Jesus' soon coming.

Stephen Haskell's main purpose in life was to win souls to Christ, and he could see that this organization could be molded into a practical soul-winning project. With his leadership and encouragement, the group was organized on June 8, 1869, under the name of Vigilant Missionary Society. The officers were Roxie Rice, president; Mary H. Haskell, vice president; Mary L. Priest, secretary; and Rhoda Wheeler, treasurer.

The work of the society expanded into a large missionary correspondence, and once Maria Huntley joined the group the women stretched their activities to include writing to people in other countries. Maria studied the French language in order to communicate more effectively with women who spoke French. Another member, Mary Martin, learned to write well enough in German to exchange letters with those who spoke that language.

From this small beginning, over time and in various stages, the Vigilant Missionary Society developed into the present-day Adventist Book Center. More detailed information on this subject can be found in the *Seventh-day Adventist Encyclopedia*.

Schools on Both the East and West Coasts

Stephen Haskell was a decisive leader and a good organizer. Once he reached a decision, he was quick to act upon it. Ella White Robinson, daughter of W. C. White and granddaughter of James and Ellen White, called him a "man of action." In 1882 this trait of character would lead to the founding of a denominational school in South Lancaster, Massachusetts, now known as Atlantic Union College.

During 1877-1887 Haskell served as president of the New England Conference as well as holding the office of president of the California Conference in the years 1879-1887. Part of that time he also was president of the Maine Conference. It's rather an understatement to say that he was a very busy man!

Meanwhile, out on the West Coast, at the 1881 session of the California Conference, plans were under way to establish a school for that area. W. C. White, son of Ellen G. White, was named as the chair of a board to set plans in motion for such a school to be opened as soon as possible. As a result, Healdsburg Academy opened on April 11, 1882, with 26 students.

It seems there was something of a good-natured race between W. C. White and S. N. Haskell as to whether a school would be started first on the East Coast or the West Coast. The West Coast won by a week, when Healdsburg Academy opened its doors in a small town north of San Francisco. However, since Haskell was president of both the New England Conference *and* the California Conference, it could be said that both the schools were his.

The new school in South Lancaster was opened in the freshly renovated carriage house that originally had been moved from the Haskell property to serve as a meetinghouse. Now it was a school, with 19 young people in attendance. That soon increased to 25. It was a high day for Stephen Haskell and the New England Conference—as well as for Goodloe Harper Bell, the teacher of the new school.

Christmas and New Year's With the Students

On at least one occasion Elder Haskell was able to spend Christmas Eve with the students. After he spoke to them about the meaning of Christmas their teachers surprised them with presents from home that had been carefully arranged around the Christmas tree. These thoughtful teachers had taken their time and energy to write to the parents, suggesting that they might want to send a gift to their child, and also suggesting some things they might need the most.

As the students opened their gifts from home, there were many oohs and aahs, followed by "Just what I needed!" The project was a great success.

The following week, on New Year's Eve, the students had a surprise of their own for Elder Haskell. They had raised funds for foreign missions and hung money on the same Christmas tree. The gifts totaled close to $400, and a large portion of it was to go to Australia, a mission field in which Haskell was especially interested.

Spreading the Message in Australia

More than 10 years earlier Stephen Haskell had heard Ellen White relate her vision of seeing printing presses in operation and naming Australia as one of the places where she had seen them. This incident had stirred within him a desire to begin the work of God in that country. Now, in 1885, he was on his way to Australia with several other missionaries.

Arriving in Sydney, Elders Haskell and M. C. Israel, an evangelist, remained there to check on facilities for their work while the rest of the group went on to Melbourne.

The two ministers made the public library one of their first stops in Sydney. There they found 13 Seventh-day Adventist books in the library catalogue. Going on to the Sailors' Home, they found not only a small library but six well-used pamphlets, each one stamped "From the International Tract and Missionary Society; Free Reading Room, 21 Boylston Place, Boston, Mass." They said it was like meeting old friends.

Much impressed with the beauty and fruitfulness of the country, Haskell observed that the people were enthusiastic in keeping up with the rest of the world. All things considered, he felt the time was right for establishing mission work in Australia. The little group of missionaries made their home in Melbourne, Victoria.

Haskell felt he should take a short trip to New Zealand to look things over and see about launching some evangelistic meetings there. He had a letter of introduction from the American consul in Melbourne to the American consul in Auckland, which would pave the way for him.

On the ship over to New Zealand, the captain told Elder Haskell that he might find a room to rent in the boardinghouse of Edward Hare. Upon arriving at the address given, Haskell found that Mr. Hare did indeed have a room for rent, and the missionary preacher was soon settled in with his books and his constant traveling companion—his faithful typewriter. He was ready to go to work. But how? This was a city with people of many nationalities and backgrounds. Clearly he needed orders from on high.

Stephen Haskell had formed the habit of speaking aloud as he talked things over with his heavenly Father, and that's exactly what he did on the day he moved into Edward Hare's house. He was so deeply engrossed in his conversation with the Lord that he didn't realize how his voice carried. The man occupying the room next door heard him—and heard him, and heard him. He was sure something was terribly wrong and ran down the stairs crying, "Mr. Hare! Mrs. Hare! That new roomer next to me is crazy. He keeps talking to himself. You have to get rid of him or I'm leaving!"

Mr. Hare hastily made his way upstairs to find out what was going on. He listened at the door and was happily surprised to hear, "Dear Lord, he's such a good man. He already believes in Your soon coming. Help me to present the Sabbath to him so that he'll accept that, too."

Edward Hare went back downstairs and told his wife, "Lizzie, that man isn't crazy! He's praying—praying for me!"

The Hares and Stephen were soon firm friends, with Stephen sharing the good news of Jesus' second coming and of the Sabbath with them. Word spread to the rest of the Hare family, and Bible studies began. It wasn't very long before Joseph Hare, the father of this large clan, made his commitment. "Elder Haskell, by the grace of God, next Saturday I'm going to do what I thought I'd been doing all my life. I'm going to keep the Sabbath of God holy." Each of the other members of the family said they would do the same.

Edward Hare, Stephen Haskell's landlord, was probably the first person in New Zealand to accept the Seventh-day Adventist faith. He lived to be 101 years old. It was into this pioneer Adventist family that Eric B.

Hare was born in 1894. He was a prolific writer and a remarkable storyteller, as well as a missionary, impacting thousands of lives.

Stephen Haskell was on hand to receive the first issue of *Bible Echo and Signs of the Times* as it came from the press in Melbourne. He also reported a newly established church of 45 members in that city

Shortly before his return to America, Haskell again visited the Hare family. After a baptism they held Communion at the Hare home, then took the necessary steps toward organizing a church. Arrangements were made for regular Sabbath school meetings. The family had become very dear to him, and it was with reluctance that he bade them farewell.

It was May 7, 1886, when Stephen arrived back in South Lancaster, where Mary was waiting for him. They had been apart for 13 months and seven days. Naturally, she was happy to welcome him home.

Mary Is Laid to Rest

Through all of Stephen's travels in the United States and around the world, Mary How Haskell was willing and content to remain at home and wait for his return. She did her part in supporting him in whatever God called him to do. She cared for him as tenderly as he cared for her. As the need arose, the Lord led in sending just the right woman to stay with her when her husband was called away.

Mary was a committed Christian. She bore her physical pain with patience and always had cheerful words for others. She and Stephen were married for about 40 years. They eventually moved to California, where Mary died in 1894, at the age of 81. In writing to Ellen White a short time later Stephen confessed, "I LOVED HER AND SHE LOVED ME." His writing in capital letters seemed to make a point he wanted clarified for all time.

Mary's Voice

In connection with Mary's death, Elder Haskell had a very disturbing experience. One evening not long after Mary died, he was feeling very lonely as he retired. He lay in bed reciting the promises of God as he drifted off to sleep. After a short time he was awakened by a light in the room. As he opened his eyes he saw a bright but shadowy light beside his bed. Then he heard Mary's voice telling him how much she loved him and how she would watch over him and comfort him from where she now was. His first instinct was to reach out toward her voice, but an inner voice said, *The dead know not any thing.* He instantly drew away from the light. Mary's voice came again, full of love and longing, urging him to recognize her.

Using every ounce of willpower and strength that he had, he said, "No! I never knew you! You are not my Mary. You are an evil spirit sent by Satan to deceive me. In the name of the Lord Jesus Christ, I command you to depart, and to trouble me no more."

In telling of this experience, Haskell wrote: "The spirit vanished. But in the going, for one brief instant, the gentle expression on that face turned to one of baffled rage, the most malignant that I ever saw on the face of any man, or in the pictured likeness of any evil demon."

Stephen was left in confusion and distress. Had he unknowingly done something wrong that had left him open to such an attempt at deception? But he no sooner had that thought than he recalled a passage he'd read many times in Ellen White's book *Early Writings:*

"I saw that the saints must have a thorough understanding of present truth, which they will be obliged to maintain from the Scriptures. They must understand the state of the dead; for the spirits of devils will yet appear to them, professing to be beloved relatives or friends, who will declare to them unscriptural doctrines. . . . The people of God must be prepared to withstand these spirits with the Bible truth that the dead know not any thing."

He felt reassured that evil spirits can and will appear to the people of God, but that he must not fear that this experience was an indication of God's frown upon him. Such things could be a test of faith in things that had been revealed in the Scriptures. And so he was able to praise God for His warnings against the enemy of all humanity and to thank Him for the sure knowledge that the dead will never bring information or comfort to the living, for "the dead know not any thing" (Eccl. 9:5).

Led by the Spirit

Traveling by train on a preaching tour in Georgia, Haskell felt impressed to get off the train at a deserted-looking station. It wasn't a scheduled stop on his itinerary. His secretary was with him, and he briefly explained to the young man that someone in that place needed help.

They got off the train and stood on the station platform with their luggage piled beside them. With no one in sight they waited, and as they waited they silently prayed.

In a few minutes a carriage appeared. The driver greeted them with a question. "Are you gentlemen expecting someone to meet you?" he asked.

Elder Haskell responded, "No, sir, we aren't. But perhaps you could tell me whether there are any Seventh-day Adventists living near here."

"Why, yes," the man answered. "There's an Adventist family about six miles down the road. They operate a little school next door to their home. I'd be glad to take you out there if you'd like."

Yes indeed, they would be most grateful for a ride to the home of the Adventist family.

When they arrived, Elder Haskell went to the door while the secretary and the driver waited. After knocking several times, he heard a faint voice telling him to come in.

Inside he found a mother and her two daughters. All three of them were sick, and the mother was quite discouraged. Immediately Elder Haskell and his companions set about to do what they could to make them more comfortable. They built up the fire, and brought in plenty of wood and a good supply of food. While Haskell was setting things in order, they told him about their self-supporting school for the neighborhood. After doing all he could to provide for their needs, Elder Haskell prayed for them. He asked the Lord to bless them and make them well and strong so they would able to open their school again.

As he glanced out the window, Elder Haskell saw children playing in the schoolyard next door, no doubt hoping that their teacher would be able to come to school that day.

"Sister Hale," he gently suggested, "how would it be if I sent the children on home and told them to come back in two weeks? You should be well and able to teach by that time."

She agreed, and she and both the little girls recovered quickly. At the end of two weeks they were able to reopen the school. Many years later the mother said that Elder Haskell's visit renewed their courage and they were able to carry on their school for several years.

What if he hadn't followed through on the impression that he should get off the train because someone in that town needed help? Where did the man in the carriage come from—the man who knew exactly where the

Adventist woman lived? Surely the angel of the Lord was guiding Stephen Haskell that day.

Whenever the call came, Stephen Haskell traveled on and on around the world, spreading the three angels' messages. In fact, he visited every continent on earth but South America and Antarctica.

Vignettes

When Stephen was 8 years old, a temperance lecturer came to his town of Oakham, Massachusetts. One of his lectures was given at Sunday school. Stephen wanted to sign the pledge, especially when he saw his two sisters and some of his schoolmates go forward. But he had quite a liking for sweet cider. He thought that if he signed the pledge he wouldn't be able to drink any more sweet cider. He wondered what terrible thing would happen if the pledge were broken, and finally got up his nerve to ask the question.

"Well," said the lecturer, "the names of all those who sign are sent to Washington. If the pledge is broken, the name is crossed off the roll."

The very thought of such a disgraceful thing was enough to make him think that if he did sign the pledge he would never, ever break it!

Then someone actually asked whether drinking sweet cider would be a violation of the pledge.

"Oh, no," the speaker assured him. "Sweet cider is the juice of worms and rotten apples; it's not breaking the pledge to eat rotten apples or drink the juice of worms."

Stephen promptly took his place in the line and eagerly signed the temperance pledge. He had suddenly lost his appetite for sweet cider.

By signing the pledge, he entered the Cold Water Army. His silk ribbon had these words:

"So here we pledge perpetual hate
To all that can intoxicate."

Stephen Haskell was about 12 when he was involved in another interesting incident. The teacher warned the children not to play on the ice when they went outside at lunchtime. Dire and certain punishment would befall anyone who disobeyed.

There didn't seem to be any reason for this order of the day. The ice was safe, having been frozen inches thick for many weeks. The boys talked it over. Should they follow this unreasonable command? Finally Stephen had it figured out.

"Look," he said, "he doesn't dare kill us. If he should give us a lickin', it wouldn't last long. And if he only bawled us out, why, that would be nothin'."

Talk about logical thinking! All the boys could follow that line of thought, and it settled the matter. They had a wonderful time on their noontime slides around the ice and took whatever punishment the teacher felt necessary to dish out. It hardly seems possible that they wouldn't have been found out, but Haskell didn't give further details.

~ CHAPTER 11 ~

Hetty Hurd:
The Woman God Wanted

A capable and independent woman in a day when most women hardly dared to think their own thoughts, Hetty Hurd went so far as to buy her own horse and buggy. She didn't like depending on someone else to take her to school or wherever else she wanted to go. She was an emancipated, self-reliant woman long before it became the accepted norm. The people in her school district were so pleased with her talents and effective methods of teaching that they offered her a contract for life—something almost unheard-of at that time.

Born in 1857, Hetty had a childhood conversion at the age of 8; but when her father died five years later, she lost interest in religion. She turned her attention to education, eventually becoming a successful district schoolteacher in Lemoore, California. Her salary of $75 a month was something else that was unheard-of at the time—most men didn't command a salary like that, let alone a woman.

In 1884 Hetty's sister, Mrs. Emma Gray, and her husband invited Hetty to go to the Oakland camp meeting with them. She agreed to go only because she liked the great outdoors and enjoyed camping. It was clearly understood that she wouldn't attend any of the meetings. The Grays were happy to have her with them on any terms.

One of the first days they were there, Hetty happened to pass by the pavilion and hear the music inside. She liked it so much that she postponed her walk in the woods and stood listening to the music. Eventually the music drew her inside, and she slid into a seat near the entrance. By the time the speaker of the hour began his sermon, Hetty had become engrossed in the proceedings. In spite of herself, she was interested in what he was saying. Over the next few days she heard not only beautiful music but sermons on prophecy and Bible truths as well. The day that one of the ministers spoke on the beauties of the new earth and the everlasting love of God, Hetty said to herself, "I'm going to be there!"

She joined a Bible study class, accepted the truths she heard, and became a member of the Seventh-day Adventist Church. Quite a commitment for one who had gone to camp meeting with the intention of enjoying only the camping! But God works in mysterious ways, and His hand was evident in Hetty Hurd's experience.

After the camp meeting John N. Loughborough and William Ings held a short meeting to encourage the new members. They were invited to sign up for "clubs" of subscriptions to the *Signs of the Times* to send to their friends or to names supplied by the ministers. Hetty wanted to do her part in spreading the gospel to others, so she ordered a club of 10 subscriptions to mail out herself.

As the short meeting progressed Elder Loughborough couldn't help noticing Hetty. He could see that she was deeply moved. Her face would flush, then turn pale. She kept clutching the back of the seat in front of her. It was obvious that she was in some kind of fierce mental or emotional struggle. At last she rose to her feet, and in a voice so earnest and filled with emotion that it brought tears to the eyes of those who heard her, she said, "Brothers and sisters, God wants me." She sat down without further explanation.

After the meeting the guest preachers went to dinner with the Grays and Miss Hurd. While her sister was putting the finishing touches on the meal, Hetty spoke with Elder Ings. She told him that her heart was filled with the love of God, and that she wanted to help His children in every way she could. She had gathered all of her valuables—gold watch, rings, chains, and other jewelry—which she placed in the pastor's hands.

"Why, thank you, Sister Hetty. Are these to pay for the papers you ordered?"

"No," she answered. "Oh, no. This is a contribution to the conference missionary society. I want you to sell these things and use the money in whatever way will help more people to learn of Christ and His great love for His children."

Hetty Hurd had taken a giant step forward in the Christian life. Only a few weeks earlier she had agreed to go on a camping trip with her sister and brother-in-law. But God was working mightily for her, and within this short time she had willingly experienced His guidance in her life—a life that was about to change dramatically.

The next year she gave up her lucrative lifetime teaching position and began 34 years of service to the church. She enrolled in one of the first Seventh-day Adventist schools for Bible instructors, held in San Francisco. Here she specialized in teaching young women how to give Bible studies. With her superb teaching skills she was a natural in giving Bible studies and teaching others how to carry out this ministry effectively.

In addition, it wasn't long before she had made a reputation for herself as an outstanding speaker. She was called to train workers in England, Africa, and Australia.

~ CHAPTER 12 ~

Stephen and Hetty Hurd Haskell: Joining Their Lives in God's Work

Stephen Haskell first met Hetty Hurd in London, where she was instructing young women in giving Bible studies. Then when a dedicated teacher was needed to train Bible workers in Africa, she was the one they called upon. As she had done when she was a young woman in California, she drove her own team of horses wherever she was needed. That took some adjustment in the thinking of the African people she worked with, for it seemed very strange to them for a woman to drive her own horses and go wherever she wanted to.

It was in Africa that Elder Haskell again met Miss Hurd. As they became better acquainted they found that they liked each other quite well and that their interests meshed nicely. Stephen, then 61, was a widower. Hetty, 37, had never been married. Their goals in life were the same: to spread the three angels' messages to all the world. And besides, they enjoyed each other's company.

The two made plans to marry when they returned to Australia. In the meantime, they each had work to complete in Africa. It was more than a year before they could answer Ellen White's call to come and teach at the new college in Cooranbong. Elder Haskell went first, for his work in Africa was finished. A bit later Hetty took passage on a different ship.

Her journey almost completed, Hetty was detained in Melbourne for three long weeks, quarantined because of a smallpox scare on board ship. While he waited in Sydney, Stephen filled appointments and held evangelistic meetings, and made all the arrangements for their wedding. When, at last, Hetty's ship arrived in Sydney, Stephen eagerly awaited her at the dock. The wedding took place in February 1897.

Meanwhile the Lord had shown Ellen White that He was sending the Haskells to assist with the new work in Australia. One of the most pressing tasks was to have the college ready to open on the appointed date. People from the community volunteered to help with the final tasks, and Hetty and Stephen arrived in time to be part of it also. Hetty and Sara McEnterfer, Mrs. White's secretary, were found on their knees, swinging hammers as they fastened floorboards firmly into place. With the blessing of God and the help of many willing hands, the school opened on the date planned.

Mrs. White said many times that Elder and Mrs. Haskell filled very important places at the school and that they had a whole treasure house of knowledge to give to the students. Mrs. White regarded Mrs. Haskell as a woman of rare ability. She wasn't afraid to put her hand to any kind of work. Tactful in her relationships with others, she never ordered them around, but worked along with them in whatever they were called upon to do. She was firm in her principles but a diplomat in the finest sense, teaching by example the love of Jesus.

More Travel

Stephen and Hetty returned to America in 1899, where they were kept busy as they attended camp meetings, held Bible institutes, and published their *Bible Training School* magazine. The paper was a great help in educating workers for God.

For a time they worked in New York City, promoting mission work. Their work there was a heavy-duty assignment and one they enjoyed. At one point the owner of a funeral home became so interested in Bible studies—after just one talk with Haskell—that he offered the use of his chapel for Wednesday night Bible studies.

Now, lest you think a funeral chapel wasn't a choice location for Bible studies, be assured that Elder Haskell checked it out and found that it gave no atmosphere of death and funerals. He was happy to accept the offer, and classes began. He even sold the man several books so that he could study on his own without having to wait for the weekly meeting.

Haskell continually thought of new ways to help people learn of Jesus. When he saw young people who seemed to have no purpose, he would say, "Come and work in the Lord's vineyard." And the next thing they knew they would be out selling literature to finance sending papers and tracts to others, or even to finance their own or someone else's education.

The Holy Flesh Movement

You may have read in *Selected Messages,* book 2, pages 31-39, about the holy flesh doctrine, which had its start in Indiana. Apparently it was S. S. Davis, the conference evangelist, who cultivated the strange teachings, and it was just a matter of time until the conference president, R. S. Donnell, accepted the doctrine. Almost all of the conference workers went along with it. The doctrine was strange (with no biblical basis), the teachings weird, and the results unholy.

Elder Haskell described their theology:

"They believe that Christ took Adam's nature before he fell; so He took humanity as it was in the Garden of Eden and thus humanity was holy, and this is the humanity that Christ had. And more, they say, the particular time has come to become holy in the same sense, and then we will have 'translation faith,' and never die."

It was Hetty's "rare ability to counsel in the love of Christ" that came to the forefront at the 1900 Indiana camp meeting. The Haskells were asked to go there as representatives of the General Conference and assess the situation. Elder Haskell had met this kind of fanaticism in the early years of the work, but it was all new to Mrs. Haskell. They both were appalled by what they witnessed. Mrs. Haskell wrote to Sara McEnterfer, secretary to Ellen White:

"We have a big drum, two tambourines, a big bass fiddle, two small fiddles, a flute and two cornets, and an organ and a *few* voices. They have *Garden of Spices* as the songbook and play dance tunes to sacred words. They never use our own hymnbooks except when Elders [A. J.] Breed or Haskell speak, then they open and close with a hymn from our book, but all the other songs are from the other book. They shout 'Amen' and 'Praise the Lord,' 'Glory to God.' . . . It is distressing to one's soul. The doctrines preached correspond to the rest. The poor sheep are truly confused."

At first both Elder and Mrs. Haskell were given the opportunity to speak at the meetings. After all, they were representing the General Conference. But after Mrs. Haskell spoke three or four times, she wasn't invited to speak again. The conference leaders easily saw that the people were listening too closely to the truth she taught in her wise and compassionate way. Now unwilling to have the Haskells and Elder Breed speak in the public meetings, Donnell warned his workers to stay away from them, for they didn't have "this experience" of holy flesh.

Both Elder and Mrs. Haskell labored for the "poor sheep," as she called them, trying to help them understand what was happening. It was a peculiar mixture of truth, error, excitement, and noise. The people were frightened and confused. One woman, a fairly new convert to the Adventist Church, told Mrs. Haskell, "You can tell by the sound whether a bell is cracked or not. Much of the preaching sounds cracked; but when you General Conference workers speak it sounds firm."

It was a frenzied, moblike situation, with lots of noise and bedlam. The noise and loud music contributed to the "Garden experience" by which they sought "holy flesh." Many people just followed blindly, while others were thoroughly disgusted with the whole affair.

Elder Haskell said that the people of that conference were not very excitable unless some kind of pressure was brought to bear on them. According to him, this holy flesh movement had a great power would draw almost anyone within its scope. When the musicians really got going, it was something to behold. Haskell wrote, "Not a word of singing could be heard from the congregation, unless it be shrieks of those who are half insane. I don't think I overdraw it at all. . . . It is enough to convert anybody to something!"

The specifics in the Haskells' letters gave a detailed picture of what was happening in Indiana, and it's understandable that there was so much concern over it. One woman was taken to the insane asylum, and Haskell was called to see another woman on the campground who was on the point of insanity. It's hard to understand fully just what went on before, during, and after that camp meeting. It seems that the people were indeed led by a spirit, but it wasn't the Spirit of God!

The Haskells were able to help many of the "poor sheep." At the 1901 General Conference session Ellen White rebuked the leaders of the holy flesh movement. Her words were clear and pointed. It was a "strong testimony," and opened the eyes of both leaders and laypeople to the movement's true character. Sincere confessions were made. The entire Indiana Conference committee resigned because they were so ashamed of their actions. The *General Conference Bulletin* of 1901 carries a statement from R. S. Donnell, who confessed his wrong in advocating the holy flesh doctrine.

Necessary changes were made in many leadership positions, and the holy flesh doctrine in Indiana and elsewhere soon shriveled and died.

The extreme fanaticism of the holy flesh movement caught a lot of people unaware. Without "hard labor," as Ellen White would describe it, there would have been many more "poor sheep" deceived and led astray. But the Haskells were the right people in the right place at the right time and were able to challenge the message. Later, with the straight testimony of the Lord's messenger, the crisis was brought under control and the deception ended relatively quickly. Satan was doing his best to create confusion and loss of souls, but the *Holy Spirit* intervened, and the *holy flesh* was terminated.

The New York City Mission

In 1901 church officials sent the Haskells to hold six Bible institutes in various areas of the country. But Elder Haskell was exhausted and became quite ill. Hetty, too, was in need of extra rest. So they spent some time at the country estate of their longtime friend Mrs. Bradford, and there they both regained strength and health. They were ready for their new assignment—setting up a mission station, not in Africa or Australia, but in New York City.

After a four-day search the Haskells found an apartment that they felt was ideal for their mission work. It was on the sixth floor of a large apartment building, high above the noise and traffic of the streets below. And further, there were so many apartments in that building and in nearby buildings that they wouldn't have far to go to make contact with many, many people who needed to know Jesus. It seemed to be the ideal place. Their work would be to conduct a training center in evangelism, as well as to work with individuals among the millions who lived in the city and who were not affiliated with any church. The new organization was called the Bible Training School, and they hoped to make the city mission self-supporting.

Mornings at the Bible Training School were for study. Elder Haskell's early-morning Bible study was held from 6:30 to 7:30, after which they had breakfast. Between 9:00 and 10:00 Mrs. Haskell conducted a Bible instructors' class for the experienced workers, then at 10:00 the beginners' class was held. In the afternoon the Haskells and their students visited people in the neighborhood. Part of the beginners' class was learning the art of selling books and papers, and Hetty Haskell gave detailed instructions. At first some of them were frightened, but they soon gained experience and confidence. One young girl, who'd never had any experience in selling anything, returned one evening with the exciting news that she had sold nine books! They all took courage from her.

Within just a few weeks of opening the New York Mission three more centers were up and running. The mission work expanded and exploded in New York City, with so many providential openings that no one could doubt that the Lord was in the work there.

It was there that Mrs. Haskell received a number of requests for written outlines of her Bible lessons. She decided to print the lessons and send them out in the mail. In this way she could expand the Bible Training School even further. And so it was that the *Bible Training School* paper was successfully launched in June of 1902.

Dancing Horses

His horses were a special joy to Stephen Haskell. During their time in New York he enjoyed getting back to South Lancaster, where he would rush out to the barn and rattle the door just to hear the welcoming whinny of his favorite horse. Mrs. Haskell wrote to Ellen White:

"You know how fond Elder Haskell is of a horse, and he has secured one that he thinks is a jewel, and it is a pretty horse, a dark bay, . . . likes to dance a little bit; but you know he would never enjoy riding behind a horse that doesn't dance once in a while. . . .

"The horse is very intelligent, kind and gentle, and we only had it a day or two until it would whinny every time the barn door rattled. Elder Haskell had made a pet of it so quickly that it knew his step before the first week was out. . . . If I didn't make a little fuss about his driving scary horses, he would be breaking colts half the time, and I think he is too old for that kind of work. He does love a horse that has a good deal of fire to it."

In California

Moving to Loma Linda in 1905, Stephen and Hetty conducted house-to-house evangelistic visits. Their years in California were both busy and exhausting. In 1908 Elder Haskell was again elected president of the California Conference. The work there was growing so rapidly that an experienced leader was needed. Haskell had served in that capacity in earlier times, and it was felt that he would be just the man for the job. Under his leadership the work moved forward rapidly.

The Women Come to the Rescue

The College of Medical Evangelists had become a reality in 1909, and it was essential that a training hospital be part of it. But how could the cost of a whole hospital possibly be financed? This was the challenge given a special committee that convened to consider the problem. The men of the committee wrestled the question this way and that. Not unreasonably, many felt that to ask the general church membership for that much money would be too discouraging, for a great amount of money was needed. And yet the plea for money was absolutely necessary. Without the money, there would be no hospital. Without a training hospital, they might very well lose the school itself.

Some committee members felt they should move forward and trust God to provide the means. Others were sure they should not incur further debt—"we must raise the money before we spend it." There seemed to be no solution. The men had explored every avenue they could think of, and now, on a sunny California morning, they sat silent and thoughtful.

It was at this point that there came a knock on the door. Four Adventist women stood there, asking if they could have a few minutes with the committee. The women were Hetty Haskell; her widowed sister, Emma Gray; Dr. Florence Keller, a returned missionary from New Zealand; and Josephine Gotzian, widow of a wealthy shoe manufacturer and generous contributor to mission needs.

These women were well aware of the pressing need for a teaching hospital for the medical school, and they had a suggestion: let the task of raising the money—estimated at more than $60,000—be delegated to the women of the Seventh-day Adventist Church. They briefly outlined the various ways in which they felt they could raise the funds.

The committee members sat in stunned silence. The four women—without further discussion—thanked the committee for their consideration, turned, and left the room. The door closed behind them.

The men looked at each other, hardly able to believe what they'd seen and heard. One by one they sat up straighter. Nodded. Smiled. That unscheduled visit gave fresh strength and courage to every one of them. The next morning the radical plan for fund-raising was presented to the conference committee, urging that the project not be stopped but that it should move forward.

The response of General Conference president A. G. Daniells was just as bold. "We do not say stop," he declared. "We say, Go on and maintain this school, and make it a success."

The four petitioners were authorized to lead the women of the church in a fund-raising campaign. Chair Hetty Haskell directed the entire effort. Seventh-day Adventist women everywhere joined together, and pooled their creativity to devise unique ways of raising money—$61,000 in all. The teaching hospital became White Memorial Hospital in 1918, so named in memory of Ellen G. White.

The End of an Era

By 1915 the Haskells were living in Nashville, Tennessee, and it was here that they received the message they had been dreading. Ellen G. White, messenger of the Lord, had died, and the funeral would be held on July 24 at the Battle Creek Tabernacle.

Previously Elder Haskell had been asked to preach the funeral sermon when the time came. He willingly accepted, preaching not with sadness but with the voice of hope and triumph. Ellen White had been faithful to her appointed work, and a crown was waiting for her. He closed with this reminder: "While we shall not see our sister any more in this world until the resurrection day, may God help us, dear friends, to be among that number that will then see her again in the kingdom of glory."

As Elder Haskell returned from the cemetery, his mind whirled with thoughts of the past and all that both Elder and Mrs. White had meant to him. At his ordination James White had given him some fatherly advice. "Brother Haskell," he'd told the young man, "always look to God, rather than to man, for directions in your work."

To Stephen that had meant that he should follow instructions from God through His messengers of old and also through His modern-day messenger. He endeavored to abide by this counsel. He was a deep student of the Word of God, and cherished the letters he received from Ellen White through the years. He didn't really know how many letters she had written him, but there are extant copies of almost 300 Ellen G. White letters written to one or both of the Haskells. He treasured every one of them. He read and reread them and had them filed in such a way that he could quickly find any specific letter he wanted.

Special Joys

On Sunday, April 21, 1918, the Haskells took part in their last major project—the opening of White Memorial Hospital in Los Angeles. It was a high point in their lives. Elder Haskell enjoyed social occasions, but didn't always take time to participate in them. He very much enjoyed the program and reception at the hospital.

As for social occasions, there was one special birthday party that stood out in his memory. In 1913 some of the faculty and students at South Lancaster Academy had planned a surprise party for his eightieth birthday—and actually managed to keep it secret. He was studying quietly in his library at home when he finally noticed that there seemed to be an unusual number of students in the house. Then he heard shouts of "Happy birthday!" and singing rang through the old house.

There were gifts, speeches, and refreshments. As he was beginning to be a little overwhelmed by all the love that came his way that evening, he saw a big red plush armchair being brought in through a window—Hetty's gift to him. That did it! In spite of his determination not to become emotional, a few teardrops did escape. What a wonderful and memorable birthday party that was.

Time Marches On

As he grew older, Elder Haskell mourned that he seemed to accomplish so little. Hetty tried to encourage him, "Stephen, when you were young you went out and preached your sermons; now you write them out and people distribute them all over the world. Back then you reached hundreds; now your books are reaching thousands."

He was somewhat comforted by his wife's words. Fortunately, he didn't know that he and Hetty had only a short time left to work together for their beloved Savior. They were in South Lancaster in 1919 when she became ill. A few weeks later she died at the New England Sanitarium.

Stephen Haskell was left alone again. Mary had died many years ago and was buried in California. Then God had brought him and Hetty together, and for 22 years they had worked in God's vineyard. Now she lay in a cemetery in Massachusetts.

Hetty Hurd Haskell was a licensed minister, leading many people to know Jesus as their Savior. She efficiently prepared countless others to do a similar work. Indeed, just as she said when she committed her life to the Lord those many years before, God did want her! And her works do follow her.

The Days Grow Shorter

As long as he had strength Stephen Haskell participated in Bible institutes and camp meetings, and continued his writing. Along with several other pioneers, he was honored at the 1922 General Conference session in San Francisco. Not long afterward, he went to live at the Paradise Valley Sanitarium. He died there on October 9, 1922, at the age of 89.

Someone once asked Elder Haskell, "Would you choose to be buried next to Mary in California or by Hetty in the East?"

His reply was "Just place me beside the one I am nearest to when I die."

He lies next to Mary in Tulocay Cemetery in Napa, California.

F. M. Wilcox, editor of the *Review and Herald,* gave this tribute to Stephen Haskell:

"Brother Haskell was a man loved by all within the circle of his acquaintance, and this circle was by no means a small one. In reality it compassed the whole earth, because Brother Haskell was known for his work's sake not alone in North America but [around the world]. . . . The influence of his godly life will roll on until the work is done."

Beyond a doubt his works do follow him.

Vignettes

As a young man, H.M.S. Richards, Sr., the well-known radio preacher, knew Elder Haskell quite well. Elder Richards once mentioned at camp meeting that he needed more songbooks for an evangelistic series he was conducting. S. N. Haskell, who was then quite elderly, was in the audience. He met Elder Richards outside the tent after the meeting, pulled out his pocketbook, and emptied its entire contents into Richards' hands. It totaled $7. That doesn't sound like much today, but it was enough to buy several copies of *Christ in Song* for the evangelistic meeting.

Haskell was always a student of the Bible. In fact, he enjoyed studying his Bible so much that he hardly dared to begin reading it while he waited for a train, for fear he would become so absorbed in studying that he would lose all track of time, and his train could come and go and he would still be sitting there in the station studying his Bible. It happened more than once!

A. W. Spalding, who knew him in his later days, described Elder Haskell this way: "He was a typical Yankee. He may have been lean and looming in the early days, but when I knew him he was massive, slow-moving, deliberate but irresistible in speech. He used those New England provincial words such as 'thutty' for thirty, and 'Lenkster' for Lancaster. His leonine head was topped by a luxuriant mane, the original color of which I never knew, but in my time gray and then white. He had a large, shovel-tipped nose, and a flowing beard."

Fortunately, photographs give a more pleasing likeness than Spalding's word picture!

D. E. Mansell, at one time a book editor at the Review and Herald, told about "the haskell," invented by S. N. Haskell: "It's a little device for pulling up tent stakes. . . . It consists of a lever on wheels with a chain attached to the end of the shorter arm. With the chain wrapped around the stake, and with the axle acting as a fulcrum, the operator pulls down on the handle and quickly and easily draws the stake out of the ground." Haskell apparently was a handyman as well as a preacher. At the time of Mansell's report the tool was still in use. An original "haskell" is on display in Founders' Hall at Atlantic Union College.

Chapter 13

Marian Davis: Book Maker Extraordinary

The little country school teacher laid aside her textbooks and became a proofreader in the office of the Review and Herald Publishing House, then located in Battle Creek, Michigan. Marian Davis loved words and had an almost photographic memory. Possessing just the skills that James and Ellen White needed as they prepared their materials for publication, they invited her, in 1879, to join them in their work. Her rare ability to recall what she had read and where she read it fit their needs perfectly. Mrs. White wrote to her son Willie, "Marian is just what we need. She's splendid help!"

Thus began a 25-year working relationship between Ellen White and Marian Davis.

It must be said that the initial work was anything but what Marian expected. She was in Michigan, and the Whites were in Texas. They were conducting a camp meeting and planned to stay through the winter, then go on to Colorado for a few weeks. Ellen White's plan was to spend the winter writing, and she asked Marian to join their group in Texas.

As it turned out, not much writing was done. Other tasks kept pressing in, and Mrs. White was able to write but little. The Texas interlude culminated in the Whites joining a wagon train headed for Colorado. Instead of literary work, Marian found herself (along with Mrs. White) cooking, cleaning up, packing, and traveling—day after day after day. They suffered through storms, snow, rain, and floods. Marian was discouraged. This wasn't what she had come to Texas for!

Then James White changed his plans and decided to attend the camp meeting at Emporia, Kansas. After that meeting there was another change of plans, and they went on to the Missouri camp meeting. Their trip to Colorado was postponed, and they returned home to Battle Creek.

Once the camp meetings were finished for the season, Ellen White's literary work began in earnest. At last Marian was doing what she so much enjoyed. What a joy it was to her to be working directly with Mrs. White's writings.

Meanwhile, wedding plans were shaping up for Marian's sister Ella. She was engaged to W. K. Kellogg, brother of Dr. John Harvey Kellogg. Marian and her brother were happy for their sister as she became the bride of the future founder of the Kellogg cereal empire.

The End of an Era

One morning in early August 1881—just two years after Marian began working with Ellen White—she sat in her office at the Review and Herald building, working on a manuscript for Mrs. White. In the back of her mind she felt uneasy. The Whites hadn't yet come to the office. Finally leaving her desk and stepping outside, she met a friend on the sidewalk.

"Have you seen the Whites?" she asked. She was dismayed at his reply:

"You mean you haven't heard? They both became very sick during the night and were taken to the sanitarium."

In a state of shock Marian rushed over to the Battle Creek Sanitarium. The report was true. Both Elder and Mrs. White were seriously ill, and Dr. Kellogg held out little hope that Elder White would survive. In spite of everything that could be done, he died late in the afternoon on Sabbath, August 6.

The next Sabbath Marian, along with 2,500 others, attended James White's funeral in the Battle Creek Tabernacle. A few days later Mrs. White, in the company of her two daughters-in-law, Mary and Emma, left for Colorado, where she would recuperate and make plans for the future.

Now that James was gone, Mrs. White needed Marian more than ever. She would depend on Marian's skills in spelling and grammar to help ensure that her writings were clear and forceful. Once Mrs. White's health was stable and she was able to return to her writing, she sent for Marian to join her in California.

At Work in California and Europe

Toward the latter part of 1881 Marian Davis and Willie and Mary White began working on the monumental task of fulfilling an action taken by the General Conference in 1880. That action was to keep the *Testimonies for the Church* in print, but to make some revisions and grammar corrections. This was one of Marian's first assignments when she arrived in California.

She also gathered other materials that needed attention, including sermons, testimonies, and letters that needed to be finished. After working all day, in the evenings Marian read each item aloud to Ellen White. Mrs. White then added or deleted whatever was needed to complete the article or letter.

After correcting these portions, Marian and Mrs. White went through the material a third time before sending it to the printer or, in the case of letters, to the recipients.

Marian knew that the materials she dealt with were messages from God, and she was careful not to change the meaning or thought of Mrs. White's writings. In fact, the writings were so precious to Marian that she began to paste copies of them in scrapbooks, which over the years grew to quite a large collection.

Uppermost in her mind was Mrs. White's proposed writing on the life of Christ, so she especially looked for statements on that subject. It was a project just waiting to come to fruition. With no working title for the anticipated volume, they simply referred to it as "the life of Christ." It was Marian's scrapbooks that made the research and assembling somewhat easier when work on the book finally began.

The day came when the General Conference Committee asked Ellen White to travel to Europe and share her testimonies with God's people there. But Marian stayed behind in California to meet the printing deadlines on certain books and articles. She joined Mrs. White in Switzerland in 1886, and although she assisted Mrs. White in many ways while they were in Europe, her main focus was on the book *Patriarchs and Prophets*—though it wasn't yet known by that title. They returned to the United States the next year.

Australia

Then in 1891 the General Conference requested Mrs. White to visit Australia and perhaps establish a school there. Although she had no particular light from God that she should go to Australia, she decided to follow her usual practice of accepting such requests unless she had specific light to the contrary. Leaving San Francisco on November 12, 1891, she took her son, W. C. White, and several others with her, including Marian Davis.

Using the trip to Europe as a rough guideline, the little company expected to be in Australia about two years. However, the two years became nine before they saw the United States again.

As Mrs. White slowly recovered from the devastating effects of crippling rheumatism, she began work on the life of Christ in earnest. Her first writings from the 1870s were enriched and enlarged with portions of her writings that, over the years, Marian had preserved in her scrapbooks.

Besides Ellen White's published articles that Marian had saved in the big scrapbooks, there were copies of letters and manuscripts. This is where Marian's phenomenal memory came into play. She could remember where she had read specific items in Mrs. White's writings and usually could quickly find just about any item she wanted. When she found it, generally it would be just what was needed to magnify the topic.

She often stacked the precious quotes on the floor, according to topic. The floor of her room frequently was covered with these stacks of paper, each carefully placed in its proper category. As Ellen White said: "Marian puts her whole soul into this work." And later on she said, "Marian greedily grasps every letter I write to others in order to find sentences that she can use in the life of Christ. She has been collecting everything that has a bearing on Christ's lessons to His disciples, from all possible sources."

The Book Maker

Calling Marian her "book maker," Mrs. White considered her an invaluable helper, collecting and arranging her writings so they seamlessly flowed together.

"She is my book maker. . . . How are my books made?" Mrs. White asked, then answered her own question.

"Marian does not put in her claim for recognition. She does her work in this way: She takes my articles which are published in the papers, and pastes them in blank books. She also has a copy of all the letters I write. In preparing a chapter for a book, Marian remembers that I have written something on that special point, which may make the matter more forcible. She begins to search for this, and if when she finds it, she sees that it will make the chapter more clear, she adds it.

"The books are not Marian's productions, but my own, gathered from all my writings. Marian has a large field from which to draw, and her ability to arrange the matter is of great value to me. It saves my poring over a mass of matter, which I have no time to do.

"So you understand that Marian is a most valuable help to me in bringing out my books."

In 1897, as they were laboriously bringing the work on the life of Christ to a close, Marian Davis wrote to W. C. White, giving him a report of how the work was progressing. She was excited to have fresh, "live" writings that would add greatly to the interest of the book. The "live" writing was material that Ellen White wrote specifically to bridge the gaps as the pages came together in manuscript form. Marian also told Willie that she wouldn't accept $1,000 for all the work they'd been able to accomplish during the previous few weeks. She began to realize the value of simplicity and compactness, and she prized it highly. She wanted as little human imperfection as possible in the book so that the divine inspiration would shine through every word.

Marian deeply appreciated the sacredness of her work. It was dear to her heart, and she often spoke of how much she loved the Lord and appreciated His love for her, and how grateful she was to Him for giving her a place in His work with His special messenger. Jesus was precious to her, and she wanted nothing to mar the work as it passed through her hands.

In 1903 Mrs. White commented: "I'm so thankful for Marian's help in getting out my books. She collects materials from my diaries and letters, and from articles published in the journals. I greatly prize her faithfulness in this work. She's been with me for 25 years and has great skill in classifying and grouping my writings."

And the Wind Blew

Marian was so busy and interested in the work that sometimes she even forgot to eat. On one of those days her stomach finally made itself heard, and she stopped to eat an apple and a thick slice of homemade bread. Then, needing to get a little fresh air and exercise, she decided to go for a walk. Once outside, she discovered that a strong wind was blowing, so she didn't stay out long.

Back inside, she was dismayed to see that the wind had blown open the door to her room. Worse than that, the open hall window had created a draft. Her precious stacks of papers were blowing haphazardly down the hall, down the stairs, and—horror of horrors—down the road! Not one stack of papers remained intact. They were everywhere—some never to be recovered.

Marian was devastated. Numb, she knelt in the middle of pages and pages of manuscript, hardly able to think what to do next.

"Oh, dear God, how could You let this happen? You know how hard I've worked on all this."

As she looked around in despair, her eyes focused on one of the papers that she had worked with just a few hours earlier: "Do not become discouraged; cast your care upon God, and remain calm and cheerful. Begin every day with earnest prayer, not omitting to offer praise and thanksgiving."

"'Hitherto hath the Lord helped us.' 'As thy days, so shall thy strength be.' The trial will not exceed the strength that shall be given us to bear it. Then let us take up our work just where we find it, believing that whatever may come, strength proportionate to the trial will be given."

After a few minutes Marian regained her equilibrium and went about the work of resorting and classifying the papers. Of course, some of the pages were gone—gone with the wind—and had to be re-created. It took several weeks of patient perseverance to undo the damage of that day. But Marian stuck with it, viewing it as another attempt by Satan to keep the book on the life of Christ from seeing the light of day.

The Work Goes Forward

When Mrs. White was not away traveling, she and Marian went over the chapters together. When Mrs. White was away, they conferred by mail. Together they began to realize there was more material than could be encompassed in one book.

In the end Marian had pulled together such a wealth of Ellen White's writings that three books were published instead of one. *The Desire of Ages* was the final title of the book on the life of Christ. The rest of that collection of materials became *Thoughts From the Mount of Blessing,* published in 1896, and *Christ's Object Lessons,* published in 1900.

A Finished Work

As the work was progressing, the faithful old typewriter that had typed and retyped Mrs. White's writings for the new books broke down. Willie and Brother Rousseau, manager of the new school at Avondale, tried to fix the machine. Seemingly held together by the proverbial baling wire, it already had been repaired one too many times. This time there was no possibility of putting it back together. There was no money to buy a new one, and the old one couldn't be fixed. It seemed that Satan had won the battle. But there was one more thing they could do.

Together Marian and Mrs. White knelt and gave their problem into the hands of the One who was directing this work. They praised Him and thanked Him for what He would do in this emergency situation.

The very next day a letter came from one of Mrs. White's friends. In it was a check for more than enough to buy a new typewriter! The letter had been mailed many weeks before, and it arrived at exactly the time it was needed.

With the new typewriter the final chapters of the manuscript on the life of Christ were finished. The priceless pages were carefully wrapped for shipment to the Pacific Press, half a world away.

Again Marian and Mrs. White knelt together and asked God for His watchcare over the precious package as it made its way across the ocean to the publishing house.

Now it was time for a real title for the manuscript known as "the life of Christ." Each of the many suggestions was considered by the author and the Pacific Press. The final choice came down to two: *The Desire of All Nations* and *The Desire of Ages,* both of which are based on Haggai 2:7: "The desire of all nations shall come." The publishing committee chose *The Desire of Ages.*

What an exciting Saturday night it was when the first copies of the new book were delivered to Sunnyside, Mrs. White's home in Australia. It was December 10, 1898, and Mrs. White and Marian eagerly opened the package from Pacific Press. The dream had been a long time in coming true, and now they were overjoyed to hold the finished product in their hands.

The End of an Era

Nine years after leaving for Australia, Marian returned home to America with Ellen White and her other helpers. It didn't take long for Mrs. White to find the very special home provided for her by God near the village of St. Helena, California. She called it Elmshaven.

As soon as they were settled, Marian began compiling materials from Mrs. White's writings for *Testimonies,* volume 5. Knowing just how to put Ellen White's writings together on any given subject, Marian was priceless in organizing the materials and putting them together in sequence.

The next task on the list was a manuscript on health. Ironically, as Marian worked on *The Ministry of Healing,* her health began to fail; she seemed to fall victim to one cold after another. She was so sick that it was necessary for her to have round-the-clock nursing care at St. Helena Sanitarium. Even after she began to get better, her recovery was very slow. It was months before she could return to her work. Because of her weakened lungs, she was in danger of developing tuberculosis. Mrs. White urged her not to work so hard, but to do just a little each day.

Little by little she improved and began some small tasks, gradually getting back to her regular work. Unfortunately, Marian soon took up her old habit of working long hours with little rest. Meanwhile Mrs. White was meeting appointments on the East Coast. One of the other workers wrote her that Marian was unwell, sad, and discouraged. She was unable to get out of bed. The work had slowed to a halt, and Marian blamed herself for lack of progress. Mrs. White wrote to encourage her, and again urged her to make regaining her health her first priority.

But Marian had fallen into depression. She worried about the books she was working on; she worried about the medical bills; she worried about past sins and mistakes. Again Ellen White wrote to encourage her to try to get well. The medical bills would be taken care of; there was nothing to worry about. Jesus loved her and would take care of her. Receiving word that Marian was growing weaker every day, Mrs. White cut short her work in the East and went home to be with her. She seemed to rally a little when Mrs. White returned, but was unable to eat. A few days later, on

October 25, 1904, she lost consciousness early in the morning. She died later that same day and was buried the next day in St. Helena Cemetery.

Who Will Fill Her Place?

For 25 years Marian Davis gathered and arranged the writings of Ellen G. White. She was an extraordinary assistant to the Lord's messenger. Shortly after Marian's death, Mrs. White reflected, "Marian was my chief worker in arranging the matter for my books. She ever appreciated the writings as sacred matter placed in her hands, and would often relate to me what comfort and blessing she received in performing this work, that it was her health and her life to do this work. She ever handled the matters placed in her hands as sacred. . . . I shall miss her so much. Who will fill her place?"

Mrs. White spent 11 more years writing and preparing books, but there was never another who could be called her "book maker." No one could replace Marian Davis, whose faithful service was "greatly prized."

Her works do indeed follow her.

CHAPTER 14

Alma Baker McKibbin: Author of the "Shoestring Books"

"You dunce! You little dunce!" shouted the teacher at shy little Alma Baker.

No two ways about it, Alma's teacher was so impatient and volatile that she was afraid of him—so afraid that her brain didn't seem to work when she was at school. At home she correctly spelled all her spelling words. But at school, most of the time, they all came out wrong. Then the teacher called her a dunce. Soon the name stuck, and "Little Dunce" became the only name he called her. The other children took it up, telling their parents that Teacher said Alma was a dunce. The parents jumped to the conclusion that Alma Baker was mentally disabled. Among themselves they sadly commented, "Oh, isn't it too bad! The oldest Baker girl can't learn. She's a dunce!"

Alma was born in 1871, and for as long as she could remember, her father had told her that someday she would be a teacher. Now she knew she was nothing but a dunce. She couldn't learn anything, She would never be a teacher. Her parents would be very disappointed if they knew she was a dunce, so she said nothing at home about her troubles at school.

Then one day Alma didn't feel well at all. She couldn't think fast enough to please the teacher, who raged at her, "If you don't spell those words tomorrow, I'm going to make a dunce cap for you, and you'll stand in the corner all day long. All the other children will say, 'Dunce, dunce, dunce.' "

But that tomorrow at school never came for Alma Baker. By the time she got home she was running a high fever. The doctor said it was pneumonia. For weeks She lay feverish and delirious, mumbling, "dunce, dunce." Her family wondered why she kept repeating that word.

As she began to recover, Alma learned that she had a new baby sister. This made three little girls in the family. She could see how much time was devoted to taking care of the baby and decided that she would make herself so indispensable to baby sister's care that she'd never be sent to school again. Never again would she face that mean old teacher. She did everything she could to follow through on her plan, and her mother was grateful for all the help.

Then one day Alma's mother mentioned that she'd soon be able to return to school. Upon hearing this, Alma burst into tears and spilled out the whole sorry story. Mother was so upset that she wept. Grandmother was outraged. "I'm glad that teacher is gone!" she said.

Gone? Gone? This was news to Alma. The old teacher had been sent away, and a gentle and beautiful young woman was now teaching the school. Alma's family assured her that this teacher would be kind to her.

And so she was. Miss Gould was one in a million. When Alma returned to school, she met her new student at the door.

"Is this little Alma, who has been so very sick? I'm glad to meet you and have you back at school," she said.

She even gave Alma a chair by her desk, asking her how far she could read in the primer.

"Oh, I can't read," said Alma. "I'm a dunce."

"Why, dear child, you are no dunce. Wherever did you get that notion?"

Hearing that Mr. Goff had said so and that he was going to make her wear a dunce hat, Miss Gould gently soothed Alma. "Mr. Goff made a mistake," she said. "You aren't a dunce. I can tell by your eyes. They're just as bright as any in this room. Class, aren't Alma's eyes as bright as yours?"

Alma was surprised to see every hand fly into the air, some children even holding up both hands. The little girl looked at her new teacher, thinking, *She isn't a teacher; she's an angel!* Alma quickly learned to read. Her greatest aim was to please Miss Gould, but she had no notion that she could read without her teacher by her side.

Alma's grandparents were Sundaykeepers, and one Sunday when Grandfather came home from church he brought her a Sunday school paper. She looked through the paper and noticed a little poem printed under a picture of Jesus. She liked poetry—her mother often read poetry to her—and as she looked at the words they began to have meaning. Before she knew it, she had read the first verse.

She could read all by herself! She read every word in the little paper. She could actually read! She quickly looked for other papers to read. When she had read everything she could find to read in the house, she ran into the kitchen and excitedly told her mother that she could read all by herself. Her mother was overjoyed—in fact, they both were overjoyed.

A whole new world opened for her when Alma realized she could read. Her mother subscribed to all the Adventist papers being published at that time, and Alma read every word of every publication that came to their home—the *Review, Youth's Instructor, Good Health,* and other publications. It was from these papers that she learned the names of the pioneer workers of the Seventh-day Adventist Church. She read Ellen White's articles with extra care.

Happiest Memories

The Baker family had heard the Advent message through Elder J. N. Loughborough while they were visiting relatives in California, but only Mrs. Baker accepted the teachings. Alma was but 6 months old at the time, and as she grew, Mrs. Baker carefully taught her daughter everything she had learned. Because of the limited time of their visit with the relatives, Mrs. Baker hadn't been baptized, but she believed the message without reservation. Mr. Baker was not sympathetic with his wife in this matter.

Alma's happiest childhood memories were of the times she was able to spend time alone with her mother. As Alma sat on a little stool, her mother read Bible stories to her and taught her the Ten Commandments. They faithfully kept the Sabbath together. She was 15 years old before they saw another Sabbathkeeper.

From the time she was very small Anna's father told her that she would be a schoolteacher and that she must go to school. She didn't have any idea what school was like, except that it was a place where one learned to read and write. They lived on a farm, and the only children she knew were her sister and cousins. Her first experience with school ended when she fell from a swing that had been pushed too high. The long recovery from the fall was followed by a bad case of whooping cough. By the time she was well again, school was out. Then the family moved to Colorado, where the "Little Dunce" incident took place.

Freckles

The time came when Alma finished the schoolwork available in the little country school. It seemed that her education was at an end. But when she was about 12, it became necessary for her grandparents to leave the farm and move into town. By going to live with them, she could continue her education. She was happy in the new school. The teachers encouraged students to ask questions and to learn all they could.

There was just one thing: her schoolmates didn't hesitate to let her know that she was definitely out of style in both dress and hairstyle. Bangs were the thing, and everybody wore them—everybody except freckle-faced little Alma Baker. (Naturally they called her "Freckles.") She took the teasing with a smile, but her feelings were hurt. She didn't like being short, chubby, and freckle-faced. She wanted to fit in, to be accepted.

She must have had *lots* of freckles, because one day the neighbor called her over to the white picket fence. He gave her a bottle of Lily White lotion. He had seen it advertised in a magazine and ordered it for her. The advertisement said that after only three applications the hated freckles would be gone forever!

"Rub it on your face every night for three nights," he told her. "Those spots will all disappear."

Alma thanked him, already thinking of her new look. She decided not to tell her grandmother—it would be a nice surprise for her.

That night she patted the lotion all over her face and went happily to bed. Next morning she jumped out of bed, washed her face, and eagerly looked in the mirror. H'mmm. There seemed to be as many freckles as usual. Thinking she probably didn't use enough of the lotion, the second night she spread an even thicker layer on her face.

Again, morning didn't seem to bring any change to the freckles. But her face burned like fire all day. In her innocence she thought simply that the lotion was taking those ugly spots out of her skin by their very roots. That night the lotion went on in an even heavier coat. Surely this would do the trick, and when morning came her face would be free of the loathsome freckles.

Searing pain woke her in the middle of the night. Her face felt twice its size, and her eyes were swollen shut. She got out of bed and managed to wet a washcloth to hold against her face, hoping it would ease the burning, but it didn't help. Grandmother heard her and came to see what was wrong.

"My dear child!" she exclaimed. "What on earth is the matter with your face?"

Alma's surprise was definitely that, although not exactly as she had planned.

Grandmother went into emergency action with warm and cold compresses for the rest of the night. Since there was no doctor in town, she asked the neighbor to take the bottle of Lily White to the druggist and see if he had something that would counteract the poison. The neighbor not only was glad to run the errand, but was very sorry for his mistake. He was frightened too. He had only meant to help the girl. He hadn't meant to cause her harm. The druggist sent some ointment that he *hoped* would be an antidote, but he couldn't say for sure.

For the next two weeks Alma's grandmother applied warm and cold compresses to Alma's poor burned face, never once scolding her for being so foolish. They could only hope and pray that her vision would be saved, but there was no way of knowing until the inflammation and swelling went down and she could open her eyes.

Grandmother wished Alma had told her how she felt about the freckles. Perhaps she could have helped her understand that it isn't good looks or a freckle-free face that makes for success—it's what's in the heart and mind.

Alma made up her mind that if she could only regain her eyesight, never again would her freckles be an issue. She would think of others and serve God in whatever way He asked of her.

After a couple of weeks she was able to open one eye to just a slit. But through that slit she faintly made out the flowers on the carpet. A few days later she was able to open both eyes and clearly see Grandmother's dear face. No harm was done to her eyes, and when she was 75 years old an optometrist told her that her eyes were 10 years younger than she was!

Healdsburg College

Mrs. Baker was determined that Alma should go to Healdsburg College in California. She sent for a school catalogue, and she and Alma studied it carefully, deciding which classes would be most advantageous.

But Mr. Baker wanted his daughter to teach in their own community. She was only 17, but she was given permission to take the teacher's examination. However, she never took it.

Alma always felt that God worked two miracles for her. First, an Adventist minister helped Mr. Baker see that a college education was a good thing; second, her father received a sizable real estate commission on the sale of a ranch.

Although he wasn't interested in religious things, Father was willing to take Alma to Healdsburg College. From his real estate commission he paid her tuition for two years. Since he didn't know whether he would have the money to pay for her sisters to go to college, he said that he expected her to help them. She was more than willing to give her word that she would. Her father kindly stayed in Healdsburg with her until she was enrolled in the college and settled into the students' home.

At long last Alma Baker was with her "mother's people." It was the long-awaited fulfillment of a dream.

Explosion in the Chemistry Lab

There seemed to be an unwritten law at Healdsburg College that one could never refuse any job allotted to him or her. Professor William C. Grainger, president of the college, called the Sabbath school the "practice school of the normal department," and students were expected to participate in it.

"In the Sabbath school," he told them, "you will learn how to teach the Bible to all ages. Begin with the children and advance until you can teach adults."

At the end of her second year Alma wrote to her father asking if she could stay one more year and finish the normal [teaching] course. His reply was brief: he thought she should come home and teach in a public school. If she wanted to stay at Healdsburg another year, she was on her own.

At this point her friend Clara Coney proposed a plan that would benefit both young women. Clara wanted to take some college work in advanced Bible. If Alma could see her way clear to help with her secretarial work, she would divide her salary with her. If the plan met with Professor Grainger's approval, they both could go to school. It did, and they continued their classes.

Things went well for several months, but then Alma began to have severe pain in the back of her neck. The pain slowly spread down her entire spine. She didn't mention it to anyone, but managed the pain as best she could, never dreaming it could be anything serious. The cause of the unrelenting pain was discovered—literally—by accident.

An explosion in the chemistry lab hurled her violently against the wall, inflicting relatively minor glass cuts on her hands and face. Within a couple of days she seemed to be better. There apparently were no other injuries. But one morning as she sat down to write a letter, she suddenly became violently ill and went into convulsions.

The doctor came quickly and after an examination reported to Professor Grainger that Alma was suffering from peritonitis and meningitis—the source of all her pain. He said she wouldn't live until morning.

That night was a nightmare for Alma and those taking care of her. She had one convulsion after another. Mrs. Grainger and a nurse stayed with her all night, one on each side of the bed to keep her from falling onto the floor.

Clara organized a prayer vigil in the dormitory parlor, where the young women gathered and prayed all through the night. Professor Grainger and other teachers prayed in his office.

God answered their prayers; the pain in Alma's spine was relieved, and she was able to rest. However, there seemed little hope that she would ever be well again. The doctor said that the best she could hope for was a short life as an invalid. Professor Grainger wrote to her father, giving him the bad news and suggesting that he come and take her home. Mr. Baker's response was that he "took a perfectly well girl to you. If she's sick, it's because of the way you Adventists live. So take care of her."

A College Diploma and a Marriage Certificate

Alma Baker and Edwin McKibbin had been "keeping company" for quite some time. He had finished college and was teaching at Healdsburg College. She had made it clear to him that she must help her sisters with their education before she could make plans for herself. "I'll wait," promised the smiling young man.

But now she was seriously ill, with a dire prognosis and no one to care for her. Edwin talked with Professor Grainger, and together they consulted the doctor. He offered no hope that she would live more than a year.

Edwin immediately said he would marry her and take care of her. The Graingers thought it a good plan. However, the doctor thought differently, advising Edwin not to ruin his life by such a step. Alma herself resisted the idea of marrying this dear man and being a burden to him. But her friend Clara asked, "Will you deny Edwin the blessing of giving? And you also have something to give—love and gratitude."

Alma thought it over and agreed. She would marry Edwin. She made a vow to herself and God: she would be a cheerful, happy invalid. If she died, Edwin would remember only her smiles, not her tears.

Professor and Mrs. Grainger opened their home for the wedding, and Alma's friends went all out to make it a wonderful, festive occasion. They beautifully decorated the parlor with roses and sweet peas, and prepared delicious refreshments to be served in the dining room.

Just before the wedding ceremony Professor Grainger officiated in another little ceremony—he presented Alma with her college diploma. Even though she hadn't completed all of her course work, he and his wife felt that every young woman should finish her education before she got married. Because of her many outstanding activities, especially with the Sabbath school work, the Healdsburg College board felt free to award the diploma.

And so Alma Baker, dressed in a pretty robe and propped with pillows in an overstuffed chair, first graduated from college, then was married to Edwin McKibbin in a lovely ceremony at the Grainger home.

Alma Experiences God's Healing Power

Edwin McKibbin lived just down the street from the Graingers. His sister Marian kept house for him and his brother Wynford. Now it was Alma's home as well, and for a few months it was a happy home for all of them. Then Edwin, who hadn't been feeling well, was advised to go to the sanitarium at St. Helena for a checkup. The news that came the next Friday morning wasn't good. Edwin had advanced tuberculosis.

On Sabbath afternoon—one day later—Alma's good friend Mrs. Hafford stopped by to visit. When she saw how sad Alma felt, she asked if she would like to attend the little cottage prayer meeting at a home in the next block. Perhaps being there would encourage her. Alma was eager to go, and willing hands carried her there on a narrow cot. She enjoyed the meeting, and felt strengthened and encouraged by the prayers and testimonies.

At the close of the meeting Mrs. Hafford made a little speech:

"We've all heard the report from the sanitarium about Brother McKibbin. I've never believed that Sister McKibbin will never be well again. I spent most of last night in prayer for her and her husband, and I'm deeply impressed that if we pray for her in faith, she will be healed. Do any of you have faith to pray with me?"

Elderly Mr. McElhany, an uncle of J. L. McElhany, who later became president of the General Conference, knelt with Mrs. Hafford beside Alma's cot. They prayed simply and sincerely. Then Mrs. Hafford took Alma's hand and said, "Sister McKibbin, in the name of Jesus of Nazareth, rise up and walk."

At that, Alma rose from her cot and walked around the room. She was healed and enjoyed basic good health from that time on, living to the age of 103.

Edwin was able to teach a couple of months in the new school year, but his hacking cough made it necessary for him to turn his classes over to Alma. She taught for him the rest of the year, while he went to stay with relatives in the milder climate of southern California. The warmer climate did help, and the next year he was able to teach the entire year.

More Sorrow for the McKibbins

It was about this time that science was becoming aware of the contagious nature of tuberculosis, and the school board decided that it was too dangerous for young people to be in a classroom with Edwin. So even though he was strong enough to teach, Edwin lost his teaching position. Without a job they had no income, so again the relatives in southern California opened their home to Edwin and Alma.

They did have something to look forward to that year. A baby boy was born to Edwin and Alma. But that happy event turned to sorrow. Their son lived only 11 months, and those were months of suffering. He was her only child, and Alma grieved deeply for him.

Challenged by Evil Angels

Although the McKibbins were living with relatives, Alma felt she needed some kind of income to help with their room and board. So she took a job as housekeeper and tutor for a family in San Diego. As Mrs. S showed Alma to her room, a strange feeling of fear came over her. That night when she tried to read her Bible she couldn't make sense of the words. She was afraid to close her eyes when she prayed. She looked around the room, but it seemed to be an ordinary room with nothing unusual about it. Yet she was restless and agitated all night and couldn't sleep.

This went on for three nights, and she was becoming ill from lack of rest. She felt she had no choice but to leave, and went to tell Mrs. S that she was very sorry, but that she couldn't stay. Before she could speak, Mrs. S asked, "What do you think of spiritualism?"

Alma's reply was thoughtful: "There are both good and evil angels. I believe spiritualism is the work of evil angels."

It turned out that Mrs. S's father was the spiritualist leader in San Diego, and she herself was a spiritualist. When Alma told her she was sick, Mrs. S knew immediately the cause of her problem. No one had been able to sleep in that particular room since a drunken father had hit and killed his sick child there. "The boy's spirit won't let anyone rest in the room," Mrs. S told Alma.

Mrs. S pleaded with Alma to stay. The family liked her and needed her. She said that they had no other bedroom, but Alma could sleep in the parlor.

Alma, however, had another idea. Now that she knew the cause of the disturbance, she told Mrs. S that there would be no further problem. She would ask God to take the evil spirit away.

Alma did only the most essential chores that day, spending most of her time praying and searching her Bible for guidance. She asked God to strengthen her faith and by His mighty power to remove the evil angel from her room. That night she knelt beside her bed and asked God to help her sleep through the night. He answered her prayer; she slept soundly and felt much better the next day. The evil influence never bothered her again.

During the next few months Alma tried to share the things of God and His Word with the family. They received her words pleasantly, but they didn't seem to be able to understand. At last the time came when Alma's husband needed her and she made preparations to go home. The last evening she was with Mrs. S and her family, the evil angel made one more effort to take her captive. As they sat at the supper table, Mrs. S seemed to be seeing something behind Alma. Mr. S asked what she was seeing.

"I see a boat on a stream," she answered. "A baby in the boat is playing with flowers, and the man is holding the oars, ready to push off. They're both looking at you, Mrs. McKibbin; they don't want to go without you."

Although Mrs. S had never seen Edwin McKibbin, she described him perfectly. But Alma's knowledge of the Scriptures and her faith in God kept her steady and secure in Him, and she didn't turn to look. She was disappointed that she wasn't able to lead the family to the God of heaven.

Soon after this experience, Alma's dear Edwin died. His courage in the Lord was strong, his last words being from Job 19:25, 26: "I know that my redeemer liveth, and that he shall stand at the latter day upon the earth: and though after my skin worms destroy this body, yet in my flesh shall I see God."

The Experimental School

After Edwin's death the Johnson family invited Alma to make her home with them. She was happy to accept their invitation, for she was totally exhausted.

At that time the importance of church schools was being presented in a series of articles in the *Review and Herald,* written by Ellen White. Alma and Mrs. Johnson read and discussed each article, believing that they had an important message for the time.

The two women decided to experiment with some of the educational principles that were given by Ellen White—namely, that "God's Word must be made the groundwork and subject matter of education." Every week the *Review* carried various articles on the subject, and they eagerly read them all.

They decided that they could try these principles while teaching the Johnson twins and their little cousin, so the parlor became a schoolroom for the three young students. This was an experiment in teaching only from the Bible, and Alma made a little primer based on the first chapter of Genesis. This gave her lessons in reading, Bible, and nature. The children already knew how to do math and figure their tithe, for they had their own garden and raised and sold vegetables. In spite of its shortcomings, Alma and Mrs. Johnson were pleased with their experiment.

The First Church School in California

No church school had yet been established in California, and there was no one to teach the teachers how to carry out the principles laid down by Ellen White. After some persuasion from Elder George Snyder, Alma surrendered to God's direction to start a school at Centralia, California. But the first words she heard upon her arrival were discouraging. The woman of the house where she was to room and board took one look at her and announced, "You won't last two weeks. No one can control some of these Centralia boys."

The prospects *were* dismal. The "school" was a little room attached to the back of the church. It was equipped with a blackboard—a 12-inch board that had been painted black—and 10 double seats, salvaged from a public school. The stove smoked; and their drinking water was in a pail with a dipper.

Approximately 30 students came on the first day of school, making up nine grades—and the ninth-grade boy was a year older than Alma. But she had no problem with "control of the Centralia boys."

Alma improvised as she taught, using materials she had on hand, and her students were enthusiastic and cooperative. Even so, it wasn't easy, for she had almost as much to do outside of the classroom as within. She wrote her own Bible lessons and outlines for nature lessons. One of the boys loved nature and brought her specimens for that class. Alma learned that the only person who didn't want the church school was the woman she stayed with. Every morning the woman would ask Alma, "Are you really going to try it another day?"

Alma's smiling response was "Yes, one day more. We live only one day at a time, you know."

In all fairness, it must be said that the school year ended much better than it had begun, although it took a case of pneumonia for Alma and a scorching letter from her friend Mrs. Johnson to the people of Centralia to help them realize that they were overworking their teacher.

Back to Healdsburg

From Centralia, Alma was called to teach the first four grades at the elementary school in Healdsburg. Also, she would be able to attend summer school, a real bonus. In many ways she was thrilled to be going back to

Healdsburg, for along with its sad memories, it held memories of many joyful and happy times.

She was happy with the prospect of teaching the lower grades, for she particularly liked teaching small children. However, prospect was all it amounted to. Before she could even make a lesson plan, she was told that since she was the only teacher present who had taught a church school, Prof. E. S. Ballenger needed her to be his assistant in the summer school. Her job: to teach 11 other teachers how to teach.

Her dream of being taught principles of teaching church school by an experienced teacher was for naught.

Teaching the Teachers

She already knew there were no Bible lessons for teachers to follow. She also knew that she needed Bible lesson outlines in order to teach her students properly. Having no other source for them, she wrote her own, sometimes barely staying ahead of each day's teaching. She put the lesson outlines into battered old notebooks, and then each day she wrote the outlines on the blackboard. Beginning with Adam and Eve, she taught her students straight through the Bible. The would-be student became the teacher, and a good one at that. Necessity is the mother of invention.

The Shoestring Bible Textbooks

It wasn't long until the teachers who came for summer school at Healdsburg College were pleading for Bible lessons of their own. Some of them sat by the hour and copied Alma's lessons from her notebooks. This was taking too much time, so Prof. M. E. Cady insisted that the Bible lessons *must* be printed.

Another challenge made the printing of the lessons a necessity.

Some of the teachers in the new Adventist elementary schools wouldn't even try to teach Bible because they had no prepared lessons. They didn't know how to prepare their own, and besides, they didn't have time. But if Bible classes weren't part of the curriculum, then what was the point in establishing church schools? How were they different from public schools?

Once again Alma Baker McKibbin was called upon to do what she didn't know how to do—write Bible lesson books and get them published. The first books were even printed at Alma's expense. The college press was a very small printshop. They didn't have much equipment, so printing was a long, tedious process. If the Bible lessons books were to be printed, Alma had to take full responsibility as author, proofreader, and business manager.

And so she found herself filling orders for the church school teachers. They needed books so badly that Alma sent out each signature—16 pages—as it came off the press. The teachers just couldn't wait for the entire book.

Of course, she couldn't give up her teaching and other responsibilities. But in addition to that, on days the signatures came from the press, evenings found her delivering them to the post office. The first book was comprised of 12 signatures. That meant that Alma made 12 mile-long hikes to the post office to mail them to the teachers. Of course, after each mailing she faced a mile-long hike back home.

Those first signatures were just the beginning of the book. Holes were punched in the pages, and Alma included a shoestring in the mailing to hold the pages together. "The other signatures will follow," she told the teachers, "as soon as they are printed." Signature after signature—they could be added to the first. Eventually they would have a complete book.

And that's how church school teachers obtained their first Bible textbooks—assembled by themselves and held together with a shoestring. That's how they got the name "the shoestring books." After several signatures had been printed and mailed, Alma had brown cloth covers made to help hold them all together. Later on her books were bound with the same brown cloth covers—but no shoestrings. Only a very few of the original "shoestring books" are extant.

Pioneer work was not easy. But thanks to Alma Baker McKibbin, the teachers in those early schools had Bible textbooks so that they could teach Bible classes to their students.

The Family Comes Calling

One Sunday morning Alma heard a knock at her front door. To her surprise, there stood her family from Colorado—Father, Mother, and little brother, Alonzo (called Lonnie), whom she'd never seen before. She was overjoyed to see them all. Lonnie was the same age her own little boy would have been had he lived. She immediately loved him as her own.

Alma's mother's health was not good. The family had come from

Colorado with the hope that in the lower altitude of Healdsburg she would recover—or if she didn't, that she might leave Lonnie in Alma's care. The next year Alma's grandmother joined them. She had lost her memory and often wandered away, trying to find her way to some previous home. They had to keep the doors locked for her safety.

After two years Father Baker became so homesick that he left the family with Alma and went back to their home in Colorado. Alma now had full responsibility for two invalids (one without her right mind) and a little boy—all on a yearly salary of $330. She said she didn't claim to be an expert in high finance, but she did claim to be expert in low finance! God blessed her faithfulness, and she was able to meet her expenses.

The Post Office Manager

A cold drizzle had fallen all day, and now continued into the evening. But in spite of the bad weather, Alma needed to mail 12 books to Australia. After providing care for her mother and grandmother, Alma wrapped and addressed the books. It was a discouraging task, for she knew that she would have trouble with the post office manager, who didn't like foreign mail because it took too much of her time to figure the postage.

The post office was a mile away, and the cold wind and rain made for a very dark night. Alma bundled up against the weather, leaving Lonnie in charge at home. She knew he would keep the fire going and put a lamp in the window for her. She was so thankful for his faithful care.

It was after 6:00 when Alma reached the post office, but the manager didn't even acknowledge her presence. Alma waited quietly until 7:00, then tried again.

"Excuse me," she said gently.

The manager didn't look up. "Can't you see I'm busy?" she growled.

"Yes, but I've come so far, and it's very dark tonight."

There was no answer. At 8:00 the woman finished all her paperwork and turned to Alma. When she saw the address, she went into a rage:

"Australia! What are these books you're sending to distant places? Who wrote them? Where are they printed?"

"Why, they're textbooks. They're Bible lessons for children," Alma mildly replied. "I wrote them, and they're printed by the college press."

The woman's hard face softened ever so slightly. She had written a few stories herself and had some respect for authors. She figured the postage, and Alma paid her. There was a brief silence; then the woman commented, "I notice that you use good English. Could you tell me where I could find a good book on the subject?"

Alma managed to reply graciously, "I subscribe to a magazine called *Correct English*. It's very helpful. Tomorrow I'll have my brother bring you some copies."

"Oh, thank you, Mrs. McKibbin. And I'm sorry it's so late—and so dark."

The kind words were appreciated, but didn't make the night less dark. Alma was sorry too!

As she trudged her weary way home, she decided to take a shortcut, but to her dismay the trail was very muddy. Plodding on, she grew so tired that she felt she couldn't lift her feet from the mud another time. She was about to give up trying when she heard footsteps on the bridge nearby. It was a big dog—a huge dog. He seemed to know that Alma was in trouble. He came as close to her in the mud as he could, seeming to say, "Grab hold; I'll get you out."

Alma rested her weight on his strong back and shoulders, and managed to pull her feet from the mud.

She was glad for the dog's company as they walked along together, her hand resting on his broad back. As they came near the large house where the dog belonged, she thought he would leave her and turn in at his own gate. But he didn't. He walked right past it, keeping by her side until they were at her gate. He stopped and looked up at her as if to say, "It's all right. You're safe and sound now."

Alma took his big head in her hands and, looking into his eyes, spoke softly to him, "Thank you. You are God's gentleman."

With great dignity the big dog turned and walked away into the darkness.

Inside the house Alma found her mother and grandmother fast asleep and Lonnie dozing over his schoolbooks. All was well, and she felt refreshed and strong again. She believed that God had sent the big dog not only to rescue her from the mud but also to restore and encourage her.

Soon afterward Alma's youngest sister came from Denver to help with the family. It was a welcome relief to know that her sick ones need not be left alone again. About a year later her grandmother died at the age of 92.

Into the Sunset Years

Healdsburg College closed in 1908. The church had always depended on the college teachers for help, and since Alma was the only teacher left there, again the church called her to do things she hadn't been trained to do. The conference president counseled her to do whatever the church asked, and he raised her salary from $30 to $40 a month. She did real pioneer work in the Healdsburg church, even filling in for the preacher. Under her leadership misunderstandings and differences that had alienated some members from one another were forgiven, and new members were added to the church roster. During this time Alma's sister married and went to live in her own home.

In 1910 Lonnie left for Pacific Union College. After their mother died and Alma's work at the Healdsburg church was finished, she went to teach at Pacific Union College. She left there in 1921 and taught at Mountain View Academy until her retirement. There she had a little home of her own, the first home she ever owned. In the 17 years she had lived in Healdsburg, she had lived in 12 different houses, one of them owned by Ellen White.

Alma McKibbin had the distinction of holding two "firsts" in Adventist history: She was the first church school teacher in California, and she was the author of the first Bible textbooks—the "shoestring books."

Alma McKibbin left a lasting legacy to the Seventh-day Adventist Church—her works do indeed follow her.

VIGNETTES

One year at Healdsburg Alma was scheduled to teach the first four grades only. She was thrilled, for she loved teaching little children. This assignment lasted a whole two weeks. Then one of the other teachers left suddenly to go to Australia, and Alma was called upon to teach his upper-grade class. A newly arrived teacher took over Alma's precious first four grades.

Unfortunately, she was given no warning of this sudden decision. Alma was simply called out of her classroom, given a brief explanation, and escorted across the hall to the older group of students. There they sat—all 50 of them! Professor Cady introduced her as their new teacher and went on his way.

Before Alma could even open her mouth—or begin to mentally adjust to this change—a young man in the seventh grade rose and politely welcomed her. In his further comments he seemed to be asking, "If you're qualified to teach us, could you please explain some Bible statements that we don't understand?"

Alma recognized the boy as being from Oakland. She knew that his mother was a Seventh-day Adventist, but that his father was a lawyer and a skeptic. Recovering her voice, she asked what their questions were.

The boy replied, "One question is about the resurrection. We don't understand how resurrection is possible, for a dead body turns to dust and becomes a part of the earth, as it was in the beginning. And sometimes a body is eaten by wild animals."

Alma sent up a quick prayer for guidance. Then she remembered that this class was interested in physiology. In the same moment she noticed two students in the room who had been in her Sabbath school class about seven years before.

She looked toward them. "This is John and Nellie, isn't it?" she began. "Strange that I should recognize them, since there isn't a particle of matter in their bodies, or in mine, that was there when we knew one another seven years ago. Identity doesn't depend upon matter but upon personality and character. The only thing we can take to heaven is character. We'll have new bodies. I'm glad that I'll have a new, incorruptible, immortal body that will never know sickness, pain, or death."

The class was well satisfied with the answer, and she was gladly accepted as their new teacher.

∽

At another time she taught a sewing class. She was surprised to learn that the boys, too, were in interested in sewing. The class made quilts for their mission project. One of Alma's favorite memories was of her 50 boys and girls enthusiastically sewing quilt blocks.

∽

It was early spring, not very warm but not really cold, either, the day Ellen White came to preach at the Healdsburg church. The members of the church there in northern California had been through what they considered a long cold winter. Although it was not what would be called a cold day, all the doors and windows of the church were closed tight. There was no fresh air coming in—the members were afraid that they might get pneumonia if they breathed fresh air.

Mrs. McKibbin tells a little story of Ellen White beginning her sermon without saying a word about having no fresh air. A few minutes into her sermon she paused and said, "It seems to be a little close in here. I wonder if the deacons would mind opening the windows on this side of the church."

The deacons were happy to oblige, and opened the windows on that particular side of the church. Ellen White resumed her sermon. After a bit she again paused.

"It seems to me that it's still a little close in here. I wonder if the deacons would mind opening the windows on *this* side of the church," she said.

So the deacons opened the windows on the other side of the church. By the time Ellen White finished her sermon that day, she had every door and window in the Healdsburg church wide open. But she had not mentioned "fresh air" at all. Mrs. McKibbin said nobody contracted pneumonia, and they all got the point. A lesson in diplomacy and tact was learned by all.

According to a little story that has made the rounds, Ellen White said something about evil angels occupying the front-row seats in church. Alma McKibbin was the source of this story. She related an instance when Mrs. White rose to speak and noticed that the front-row seats were empty. She said, "Brethren, if you do not occupy these front seats, the evil angels will. Do you want the evil angels to come between you and me and take away the message that is for you?"

Everyone immediately moved forward.

Jim Nix tells of his interview with Mrs. McKibbin about 70 years after the death of her husband. He asked about her husband and baby, and her eyes sparkled with love and remembrance as she talked about them. She said how wonderful it was to anticipate being with them throughout eternity in the heavenly kingdom. She loved Edwin for marrying her and taking care of her in her illness. She never considered marrying again; her mind was fixed on the soon coming of Jesus, when she and Edwin and their baby would be reunited and live with Him forever.

~ CHAPTER 15 ~

Stephen Smith: The Unwanted Testimony in the Trunk

To say he was hard to get along with is putting it mildly. He was unfriendly, and his volcanic temper erupted much too often. Stephen Smith was known around Washington, New Hampshire, as a "hard-bitten New Englander who liked nothing better than a good squabble." He was known to say that he came to church to "rap on the hive to hear the bees hum."

Stephen Smith accepted the third angel's message in 1850, and he and his wife and children became active members of the Washington, New Hampshire, church.

However, he soon began to undermine confidence in the leaders of the Advent message; he felt he had received "new light" through one of the offshoot movements that had begun to spring up. James and Ellen White were his favorite targets. Even though he had seen Mrs. White while she was in vision, it wasn't enough to convince him that her messages were from God. He wanted nothing to do with her—except, of course, to use her as a whetstone for his critical spirit.

In late October of 1851 a conference was held by the Advent believers in Washington, New Hampshire. About 75 people, including Elder and Mrs. White, came from surrounding areas as well as from other states. Stephen Smith wasn't shy about proclaiming his new views.

On Sabbath afternoon, as the sun sank low in the sky, Mrs. White was given a vision concerning the members of the Washington church. Afterward she spoke frankly about what God had shown her, and all who heard accepted the counsel as coming directly from God—all, that is, except Stephen Smith and E. P. Butler. During the entire meeting Smith was so vitriolic in renouncing the visions and the work of James and Ellen White that the entire gathering felt it was necessary to disfellowship him until such a time as he could come into harmony with the believers.

The next year he seemed to have a change of heart, and he was accepted back into the group. But that didn't last long either. He believed in the Sabbath, but had no use for the visions given by God. As a result, he was ready for any offshoot party claiming to have something new.

He first joined the Messenger Party, but it soon fell apart. Then he went with the 1854 time-setting group until it collapsed. After that he was off with the Marion Party and their no-organization, no-sanctuary, no-Spirit of Prophecy teachings. The fledgling church clearly recognized the true nature of these dissident teachings, for the Lord showed them to Ellen White in vision. But Stephen Smith felt he was above such warnings and counsels.

In spite of his hatefulness, the Lord still loved Stephen Smith. In fact, He loved him so much that He gave Ellen White a vision so that Smith might understand his danger.

She carefully wrote out everything that had been shown her, and closed the letter with an appeal to Stephen Smith to return to the Lord. Then she mailed it to him.

A few days later the post office manager handed him the letter. He recognized the handwriting and knew it held a testimony for him.

How dare she! Mrs. White had written him a testimony when he didn't want any testimony! His violent temper sent the blood rushing to his head as he fought to hold back his anger. Determined that he would *not* read that letter, he shoved it into his pocket and angrily strode home. As he went into the house, he saw the trunk over in the corner. He was so furious that he could hardly control himself, but at once he knew what he'd do. Lifting the lid, he pushed the unopened letter into the bottom of the trunk, covering it with quilts and odds and ends. He slammed the lid with a bang, and turned the key in the lock. There! That would take care of the unwanted testimony!

For 28 years that testimony lay in the bottom of the trunk, unopened and unread.

If possible, Stephen Smith became even more bad-tempered. Someone who knew him well said, "Stephen Smith had the most withering, blighting tongue of any man I ever heard. He could say the meanest things in the meanest, most cutting way of any man I ever met."

We can be sure that Mrs. White and the Spirit of Prophecy came in for a good share of that withering tongue.

Stephen Smith spent what should have been the best years of his life making life miserable for everyone else. In spite of her husband's attitude, Mrs. Smith remained loyal to the church, but she and the children led a most unhappy life.

The years rolled by. Stephen Smith's hair turned white, and his shoulders became stooped. Then one day in 1884 he passed through the parlor and saw a copy of the *Review and Herald* on the table. Looking around furtively to see if any of the family happened to be in the house, he picked up the paper and paged through it. He noticed the name of Ellen G. White on one of the articles. He took time to read it, and when he was finished he thought, *That's the truth!*

The next week there was another copy of the paper on the table. He read it, and when he finished the article by Mrs. White, he again said to himself that the article spoke the truth.

As the weeks passed, Stephen Smith continued to read the *Review,* and possibly other church papers. Slowly he began to soften in his words and attitudes. His wife and neighbors noticed the change. Did his wife purposely leave the *Review* on the table week after week? Did she realize he was reading it?

In the summer of 1885 the announcement was made that Eugene Farnsworth was coming back to hold revival meetings in his old home church at Washington, New Hampshire. William Farnsworth, his father, had accepted the Sabbath in that same little frame church in 1844. In that church Ellen White had delivered a public rebuke to William that led him to give up tobacco and become the Christian he professed to be. That act had its effect on Eugene, and he became a minister—a local boy who made good. There was a great deal of excitement as word got around that he was coming to hold meetings.

Smith had liked Eugene when he was a boy. He thought it might be a good thing to see him again and hear him preach, and on the appointed day he was in the congregation.

When Elder Farnsworth finished his sermon, Stephen Smith stood to his feet. Farnsworth was well aware of Smith's up-and-down experience, and he hardly knew what to expect—probably more criticism. But what he heard was quite different.

Stephen Smith spoke of the past, confessing his involvement with the offshoot parties and his opposition to church organization and almost everything else. He'd seen those offshoots disintegrate and fall apart. He admitted that he and others who had opposed the work of the church had come to nothing, and that those who held fast to the faith had grown spiritually and were closer to God.

Now, almost at the end of his life, he had discovered that more than anything else he wanted to be in harmony with the Advent people.

The congregation was amazed to hear such words from this man. They knew all about his past, and while they wanted to believe him it's understandable that they may have been skeptical.

After his public confession, Smith began to think about his past. In time he remembered that letter he'd stuffed in the bottom of the trunk. It had been years since he had even thought of it, and for the first time in all those years he wanted to know what it said.

With hands that trembled with age and anxiety he turned the trunk key in the lock and swung the lid up. He reached way, way down to the bottom, searching for the feel of the paper he had so angrily placed there those many years before. When at last he held it in his hands, he just looked at it. Abruptly he sank into a nearby rocker and began to read the yellowed paper, now brittle with age.

Tears flowed down his face as he read a detailed description of what his life would be if he continued in the path he had chosen. There was a precise picture of bitterness and disappointment—exactly what his life had been, for he hadn't changed his harsh attitude.

The letter closed with an earnest appeal to return to God.

The next Sabbath morning Smith was back at the church. Though Elder Farnsworth knew nothing of Smith's experience during the past week, he had chosen to speak on the Spirit of Prophecy. He had hardly finished his sermon before old Mr. Smith rose from his seat. What a testimony he had:

"I received a testimony myself 28 years ago, took it home, locked it up in my trunk, and never read it until last Thursday. I didn't believe the testimony was true, although I confess that I didn't know a word that was in it. I guess I was afraid to read it for fear it would make me mad. But I was mad nearly all the time anyway."

Finally he admitted:

"Brothers and sisters, every word of that testimony is true, and I accept it. I have come to the place where I finally believe the testimonies are all of God. And if I had heeded the one God sent to me . . . it would have changed the whole course of my life, and I would have been a very different man. . . . The testimonies were right and I was wrong.

"Brethren," he concluded, "I'm too old to undo what I've done. I'm too feeble to get out to our large meetings, but I want you to tell our people everywhere that another rebel has surrendered."

That letter lay in his trunk all those years with a message God sent to save him from a life of anger and hate. A message unread and unheeded. According to his own testimony, if he had read and taken the message to heart, it would have changed his very being, and he would have lived a godly, useful life.

Through His marvelous grace God accepted Stephen Smith when he finally surrendered to Him. Smith lived his later years in a far better way than he lived those 28 miserable years when the testimony lay in the trunk, but sadly the best years of his life were wasted in bitterness and hate.

Vignette

Willard Saxby

A man named Willard Saxby also received a testimony from Ellen White. But the outcome was very different from Stephen Smith's experience.

It was at camp meeting that Brother Saxby received the testimony Ellen White sent to him, detailing some of his most grievous character flaws. It was hand-delivered and personally read to him by Elder A. During the reading of the testimony Brother Saxby objected four times, saying, "No, no; that's not so!"

Elder A suggested that if he were to say it was so, then the Lord would help him to see that it was so.

Saxby then took the letter to his camp meeting tent, where his wife had already gone to bed. He was so agitated that he insisted on reading one paragraph that concerned the two of them. After he read the paragraph, he kept repeating that it wasn't so. His wife sat straight up in bed, pointed her finger at him, and earnestly assured him, "Willard, that *is* so! It most certainly is so!"

He began to think seriously that if his wife said it was so, and Elder A said it was so, and most of all, if the Lord Himself had sent the message through His messenger, it must be so.

So Willard Saxby accepted the counsel of the Lord, saying, "Three against one. It must be so!"

How wonderful it would have been for the work of God had Stephen Smith had the same attitude.

Chapter 16

John Norton Loughborough:
Part 1
"Fear God and Give Glory to Him"

Even in his old age John Loughborough vividly remembered one cold, crisp night as his family rode to church in the sleigh, the harness bells jingling merrily as the horse trotted along. He remembered how the frosty air felt on his cheeks and the sound of the snow crunching under the runners of the sleigh. He remembered the text that the preacher had read that night, "Fear God and give glory to him; for the hour of his judgment is come," making it clear that the time of the judgment was near at hand.

As the sleigh skimmed along, John overheard one of his cousins make a joking remark about the coming of Jesus. His grandfather also overheard the remark, and in his gentle voice he said, "Young man, you'd better be careful how you treat this subject before you know what it is."

John also remembered that as the crowd of worshippers came out of the church that night, they saw a sight that left them awed and wondering. It was a band of light, about as wide as the moon, stretching across the heavens. With the almost-full moon shining brightly and the band of light casting a mysterious glow across the sky, it was an unusual and impressive sight. Standing quietly, the people looked at it for a long time. They remembered the prophecy in Joel that said, "The sun shall be turned into darkness, and the moon into blood, before the great and terrible day of the Lord come." Surely this was a sign that Jesus was coming soon.

The boy who had made the jesting remark looked into the night sky with solemn amazement. With a trembling voice he confessed, "Uncle Nathan, you and the Adventist preachers are right. This is a sign that Jesus is coming soon."

The Adventist preacher continued his lectures on the second coming of Christ, and the Loughborough family attended every service. With renewed interest and hope the group now eagerly looked forward to October 22, 1844, the date that some Bible students and preachers had set as the time when Jesus would appear in all His glory.

But along with many others, the Loughborough family was greatly disappointed when October 22, 1844, came and went, and Jesus did not appear.

However, as more light came to the believers, young John was happier than he'd ever been, for his trust and hope were in Jesus and His promises.

A Christian Family

John Norton Loughborough was born into a Christian home on January 26, 1832, in Victor, New York. Although they weren't ordained ministers, both his father and grandfather were lay preachers in their local Methodist Episcopal Church. They were instrumental in establishing a small congregation and building a little church in their community.

One of John's earliest memories was of family worships, morning and evening. There were five children in the family, and his father read and explained the words of the Bible so that even the youngest of them could understand. The children enjoyed going to church, but their mother was often sick, and on those days when she couldn't take them to meeting, they played church at home. Little Johnny always did the preaching and the praying.

John's father, Nathan, was not only a lay preacher, but an accomplished carpenter, making cabinets and chairs, as well as building houses. He also was the only coffinmaker in the entire community. Sometimes after completing his church work late in the evening he would arrive home to find an order for a coffin that was needed the next day. Of necessity, he would spend the rest of the night making the coffin, for burials took place within a short time after death.

At the age of 35 Nathan Loughborough contracted typhoid fever. The standard treatment at the time was to bleed the patient and dose him with calomel. No water or fresh air was allowed. It's little wonder that the beloved father didn't survive the medical care. Records indicate that about 2,000 people attended his funeral.

John was 7 years old when his father died. To help his ailing mother cope with her burdens and the other four children, Johnny was sent to live with his grandfather, who owned a farm not far away. Grandfather had plenty of work to keep the youngster busy, and he soon came to enjoy riding the plow horse. From his perch high on the horse's back he could look backward and see the plow turning the fresh black dirt. He liked living with his grandparents, and even though he was young and small for his age, he didn't mind the work.

Some of the townspeople weren't very friendly to the Methodist Christians, occasionally even causing them real trouble. One day Grandfather Loughborough found several lengths of his fence torn down and the neighbor's cattle enjoying a good lunch on his corn. But being the Christian gentleman that he was, without saying a word Grandfather herded the cattle back where they'd come from. While the owner and his sons stood by laughing and making crude remarks, he made the necessary repairs to the fence. Then he went into the house and prayed for these men who had let their cattle into his field.

On another occasion the family returned home from church to find that their heavily laden cherry trees had been mutilated by saws and axes. It was the best crop of cherries in years. Weeks later the mangled limbs, with their now-rotten load of cherries, were found in a heavily wooded area a half mile away. The same thing happened with pears on a large pear tree; even worse, the pears had been promised for sale. Grandfather made no public accusation, but prayed earnestly for these men who were so determined to persecute him. Eventually his Christian kindness won out, and the men became his staunch supporters.

John Loughborough's values in life were formed by those he saw lived by his family: "Do unto others as you would have them do unto you."

Education Is Necessary

Feeling strongly that his grandson should have a good education, Grandfather Loughborough laid plans for John to get the needed schooling.

John was eager to go to school, and he also wanted to become a skilled craftsman. One of his cousins had a violin, and John thought he would like to learn how to play it. Having no money to buy one, he fashioned his own, using a beech board to shape the body of the delicate instrument. The violin was as well proportioned and balanced as those sold in music stores. Its tone must have been quite good, because a doctor who lived in the little town bought it from him for a substantial sum.

John's carpentry skills were more acute than his musical skills, and he never learned to play very well.

At 15 John went to live with his brother and his wife in order to obtain the good education that he and Grandfather had designed. The plan was for him to work in his brother's carriage shop during the summer and go to the local high school in the winter. But the plan failed. Seven months later his brother closed his shop and moved to Adams Basin, New York, where he worked with another carriage maker.

This left John without a job, so he went back home to live with his mother and go to high school there. He did janitor work—swept classrooms, built fires, and rang the bells—in exchange for his tuition.

Sometime after his return home, his uncle Norton came to see him.

"John," he said with a smile, "I'm going to visit your brother over in Adams Basin. How would you like to drive over there with me? We'll stay for the weekend."

"Oh, Uncle Norton, I'd like that first-rate. I'm sure Mother won't mind; I'll go and ask her."

So it was that John and Uncle Norton went to Adams Basin. On Sunday John eagerly went to an all-day meeting that was being held by Phinehas Smith, an Adventist preacher. John was so interested in what he heard that he changed his plans so he could attend the meetings being held the following weeks. He arranged for a job in a local blacksmith shop, where he was promised an apprenticeship in carriage building. He could earn his room and board working in this shop and still be able to attend the Adventist meetings.

John went back home to pack his few belongings and with a certain amount of sadness said goodbye to his mother. He had a job, but would he be able to attend school as well? Determined to follow the Lord's leading—and for now this seemed to be it—he returned to Adams Basin to take up his new work.

As he went about his chores in the blacksmith shop, John kept his

Bible near him so he could study in his spare time. He listened to Phinehas Smith's preaching in the evening and the next day reviewed all the texts the minister had used. When work was slack, he often went into the shed behind the shop and prayed. He felt certain that God wanted him to spread the good news of Jesus' soon coming, and it wasn't long before he made the important decision to commit his life to God. He and another man were baptized by Evangelist Smith in a deep channel of water, joining the first-day Adventists.

Using the old-fashioned bellows and the anvil hammer was hot, heavy work in the blacksmith shop, but John faithfully did his part in fulfilling his agreement with the man who had hired him. As customers came into the shop John tried to talk to them about the Bible truth he was learning. Some were interested and responsive, but most just made it a joking matter.

The blacksmith shop was located near the Erie Canal. Behind the shop was a shallow pond created by the overflow of canal water as the boats passed. This pond of dirty water was the perfect breeding place for millions of malarial mosquitoes. To say it was an unhealthy environment is to put it mildly.

The blacksmith had promised John an apprenticeship in carriage making. But promises, promises—that was all he ever got. During the time he worked there not one carriage came in for repair. He learned nothing about carriage making, an art that he had hoped to perfect in order to have a trade.

After working for three months, he finally broke his contract with the owner for failing to deliver on his part of the agreement. His total wages for those three months was room and board and a well-used calfskin apron.

It seemed at the time that everything was against him. He wasn't well, and he was thoroughly discouraged. There was nothing to do but go home to his mother. Within a few days he sweated and shivered in the grip of the dreaded malaria. His mother nursed him through the severe chills and fever, which came often, and prayed with and for him.

With each attack of the chills and fever he felt strongly impressed that he needed to tell others the wonderful truths he'd been learning from the Bible. When the chill had passed, he would say to himself, "How can a 16-year-old boy preach? Who would listen to him?"

And then one day there came two very hard chills, one after the other. He was sure he would die. As he prayed, he heard a voice telling him to go out and preach. He answered:

"Lord, break these chills and fever, and I'll go and preach as soon as I'm strong enough to do it." After that day there were no more chills, and he slowly began to recover.

He had made the promise to go, but how would God make it possible for him to preach? He didn't have any money, or even suitable clothes for standing up before people and preaching. His long illness left him debilitated and frail. He didn't have the strength to cut wood or do other heavy work to earn money, but he did little odd jobs as he was able.

Time passed. On days that John was too weak to work, he studied his Bible and wrote sermons. He wanted to begin preaching as soon as he was able. One day when he felt a little stronger his neighbor gave him a job sawing wood, for which he was paid a dollar. This dollar was the only money he had, though he had done his best to earn and save,

He felt he *must* preach about Jesus' soon coming; he *had* to preach! But he still had no money and very little clothing. How could he do it?

Knowing of his desperate desire to spread the gospel, the same neighbor who had given him a job gave him a vest and a pair of pants. But the neighbor was a big man, six feet tall, and John Loughborough was not very big or tall. The trousers were seven inches too long. So seven inches were cut off, but still the pants didn't fit—they were too big all over.

But John put them on and was happy for them. His brother gave him a coat, also too large. Cut off and overlapped in front, it became a double-breasted overcoat. It would have to serve as a suit coat as well.

Dressed like this—pants too long, vest hanging from his skinny shoulders, a cutoff overcoat for a suit coat, with the sleeves hanging down over his hands—John Loughborough was ready to go out and preach.

Only one person in the world—his brother—knew of his decision to begin preaching. He plan was to begin about 30 miles from home. He reasoned that if he failed perhaps no one in his own town would ever hear about it. But if the Lord blessed his efforts with success, he would know he was doing God's will.

His Father's Friend

Then one day Caleb Broughton,* an old family friend, came to visit him. "John," he asked, "what are you going to do this winter?"

"The man I worked for during the summer wants me to come back to work in his carriage shop," John said respectfully. "But he hasn't even paid me for the work I did for him then. I think he's a poor pay risk."

"All right," returned Mr. Broughton, "but what are you going to do?"

"Well, my brother has asked me to stay with him and go to school, doing chores for my room and board."

"Yes," repeated Mr. Broughton, "but what are you going to do?"

"Well, Brother Broughton," John replied in his careful way, "I've decided to go over west of Rochester and try to preach."

At last! At last he had spoken of his cherished dream. He fully expected his friend to laugh and say it sounded like a lot of foolishness to him.

He was surprised to look up and see a wide smile on Mr. Broughton's face. "Thank the Lord!" he exclaimed. "That's what I've expected you to do—to become a minister of the gospel."

Then he told John a story he'd never heard before:

"One day I was visiting at your father's house. You weren't quite 2 years old, and you were playing there on the floor with your wooden blocks. Your father was telling me his hopes for your older brother and sister. He was sure your brother would become a good mechanic and your sister would make a wonderful teacher.

"I asked, 'Nathan, what's the little fellow going to be?' In a serious voice he answered, 'Brother Broughton, that little fellow is going to help sound the gospel trumpet.'

"Now, John, I've been watching you all these years, and I can't tell you how glad I am that you're going out to preach."

After a little thought he asked, "How are you fixed for money? I know you've been sick."

John told him he had a dollar. That would pay his way to Rochester, and he would have 25 cents left. He'd walk the rest of the way to Kendall Corners, New York, and begin work there.

Mr. Broughton pulled $3 from his pocket and handed it to John. "This will help you on your way."

John was much encouraged by the man's kind words as well as his practical expression of confidence by the gift of money. This gave him the needed assurance that he was on God's mission to preach the gospel.

Beginning to Preach

It was a momentous day—just before his seventeenth birthday—when John boarded a train for Rochester. He had a package of first-day Adventist papers, worth $5, that he hoped to sell in order to help with his expenses. Upon arriving in Rochester, he walked 10 miles to his brother's home in Adams Basin, where he spent the night. His brother gave him a small satchel in which to carry the papers, his Bible and hymnbook, and the few personal items he had.

What courage it must have taken for young John Loughborough to walk the 10 miles from Rochester to Adams Basin, then another 15 miles to Kendall Corners. It was the middle of winter, and his clothing was far from warm. How bitterly the sharp wind must have cut through those too-big trousers and thin coat. But in later years he couldn't recall that he had been especially cold or uncomfortable. Hardship was a way of life in those days, and he was excited to be on his way to preach the message of Jesus' soon coming. What was a little cold or discomfort when such a calling lay before him!

His First Sermon

Securing permission to use the small Baptist church in Kendall Corners, New York, John Loughborough preached his first sermon on January 2, 1849. Word had circulated in the community that "a little boy" was going to preach. The church was full, each person eager to hear the young preacher's sermon on the Garden of Eden, Adam and Eve's disobedience, and their agonizing loss because of their wrong choices.

As John looked into the earnest faces in the audience, God gave him the assurance that He was using him, and the Holy Spirit impressed hearts. Neither his age nor the comical way in which he was dressed seemed to detract from his message. Perhaps the Lord caused the eyes of the people not to notice how he looked. But it probably was a good thing that he didn't know until later that there were seven ministers in the congregation that night.

He preached at the little church two nights, carefully quoting Scripture to prove his points. The people eagerly accepted what he had to say, for they could see that he proved everything from the Bible. But the local ministers didn't like what was happening, and at the close of the second meeting there was an announcement that singing classes were beginning the next night—in the church. The church no longer would be available to the young preacher.

Now, some in the audience knew that the singing classes had been quickly arranged for the purpose of closing down the meetings, and they promptly invited John to hold his meetings in the schoolhouse just five miles south. One of the trustees lived near the school, and he invited the young preacher to stay with his family and continue the meetings. Immediately accepting the invitation, John asked the trustee to make the speaking appointment for the next evening.

The following morning as John was about ready to leave for the schoolhouse, he received a message that some of the village people wanted to talk with him. When he arrived at the gathering place, he found quite a number of people discussing the meeting of the night before. He enjoyed talking with them and answering their questions. Then the Baptist minister came in. He looked John over, observing his much-too-large clothing, including the cutoff overcoat that served as his suit coat. "You had a large attendance last night?" he asked with a sneer.

"Why, yes," John replied, "we did. And the people seemed very interested."

The minister suggested that they probably were curious to hear a boy preach. Then he went on: "Say, Mr. Loughborough, did I understand you to say that when a person dies he doesn't go to heaven?"

"Yes, that's right. That's what I said."

Now, this was a newly discovered truth from the Bible, and not all Adventists believed it yet. But John Loughborough had studied it carefully for himself, and he knew it to be truth from God.

"Well, young man," the minister responded, "how do you explain the text that says 'These shall go away into everlasting punishment, the death that never dies'?"

"Sir," the "boy preacher" replied respectfully, "one half of the text you've quoted is in the Methodist hymnbook and the other half is in the Bible. The expression 'death that never dies' is not in the Bible."

The minister insisted that there was a text that read as he had said and that it could be found in Revelation 25.

To the great delight of all the people who stood listening to the dialogue, the younger man courteously answered, "My good sir, there are only 22 chapters in Revelation. Your text must be three chapters outside the Bible!"

The minister drew himself up to his full height—and he looked very tall indeed beside "the boy." Then he thundered, "I tell you it *is* in the twenty-fifth chapter of Revelation. Give me your Bible and I'll show you."

He took the Bible and began turning the leaves of the Old Testament. At last he asked, "Um, where is Revelation?"

"Look near the back cover of the Bible," John quietly told him. "Revelation is the last book of the Bible, and as you can see, there are but 22 chapters."

Confused, the minister looked at it for a moment and then remarked, "Well, I'd like to talk to you longer, young man, but I have an appointment." And he quickly left the room.

He had told the people that he would show the "boy preacher" in about two minutes where he was wrong. The minister may have read many books, but apparently he didn't have much of an acquaintance with his Bible.

From First Day to Seventh Day

In 1851, when John was 20 years old, he married Mary J. Walker. They soon moved to Rochester, New York, where he worked as a house painter. He also was the lay minister for the Advent believers in the area who still worshiped on the first day of the week. He had three churches, two of them several miles from Rochester, and he visited at least one of them every weekend. His time was spent in painting houses during the week and visiting and preaching on Saturday and Sunday. He also sold Arnold's patent window-sash locks, which brought in enough money to live on and pay his traveling expenses.

During this time John had been led to study what the Bible says about the sanctuary of God and to look for biblical evidence for keeping Sunday holy. One night he had a dream in which he seemed to be in a meeting in a smoke-filled, poorly lit room. From there he could see a clean, well-lit room, filled with people who had Bibles in their hands, eagerly enjoying the Word of God. He also saw a chart depicting strange-looking beasts. Beside the chart stood a tall man who seemed to be devoted to God's

Word. In his dream John went into the bright room. He then awoke with the impression that he soon would find great light on the sanctuary question that he had been studying.

On a bright September day in 1852 Jonathan Orton, a good friend of John's, invited him to a meeting being held that evening. Orton had already decided to cast his lot with the Sabbathkeepers, and he wanted John to come to that same conclusion through his own study of the subject.

When he invited John to accompany him, Jonathan mentioned that two of John's congregations had joined the "seventh-day people," and that a Mr. Andrews was lecturing on the seventh-day Sabbath. He suggested that perhaps John could raise questions about this new message by sharing the texts he had gathered that showed that the law had been abolished. As he thought about it, Loughborough decided it was a good plan. He and his friend Jonathan went to the meeting together.

When they entered the meeting room, John was surprised to see the very chart he had seen in his dream. Then he recognized J. N. Andrews as the man he had seen. As Elder Andrews presented his points on the seventh-day Sabbath, he used the same texts that Loughborough had on his list for keeping Sunday. One by one John was forced to cross off the texts, for Andrews proved his points by the very texts John had amassed to prove the opposite view.

By the time the evening ended, John Loughborough was convinced that he had been very much mistaken in teaching that the moral law had been abolished. He discovered that there were two laws—the ceremonial law, pertaining to sacrifices and other ceremonies, and the moral law, as given in the Ten Commandments. It was the ceremonial law that had been abolished, not the Ten Commandments.

He later described that evening as being something akin to a magnificent view into a beautiful expanse of light. He was more than grateful to God for leading him, and he felt certain that there was much more to learn. Finishing up his appointments for the first-day Adventists, Loughborough then joined the little company of Sabbathkeepers in Rochester. The group met at 124 Mount Hope Avenue, the place where the Sabbathkeeping Adventists printed their paper and where the workers lived.

Jonathan Orton

Jonathan Orton, the man who had invited John Loughborough to the meeting held by J. N. Andrews, made his livelihood by driving a hack—a horse-drawn taxi. One evening in March 1866 he arrived home and called out to his wife that he was on his way to the barn with the horses. Their son, Alva, was to be married the next Sunday, and as she waited for Jonathan to return to the house to finish some last-minute wedding chores, Caroline felt a curious mixture of happiness and dread. Happiness for her son's approaching marriage and some unknown fear for the future.

After waiting for about 20 minutes for her husband to come in, Caroline went to the barn to see what was taking him so long. There she found him, the right side of his head and face crushed and bleeding. In answer to her screams the neighbors quickly came and carried him into the house. The doctor came. The police came. But there was little the doctor could do, and Jonathan Orton died about midnight.

Instead of a happy wedding on that much-anticipated March Sunday, the Orton family buried their husband and father.

John Loughborough did his best to comfort the family. He reminded Caroline of Ellen White's graphic vision the previous December.

James and Ellen White had been at Our Home on the Hillside, a health retreat in Dansville, New York, where James had been sent to rest and for recover from a severe stroke. However, Ellen wasn't satisfied with his progress, and she was taking him back home to Battle Creek. He was still very feeble and weak, and travel was difficult for him. So they broke their trip home with a stay in Rochester, where the church members banded together to pray for him twice a day. Jonathan Orton was one of the Rochester church members who prayed for James White's recovery.

During a season of prayer on Christmas Day James received the marked blessing of God. Afterward, Ellen White was given a vision in which she was instructed to warn the Adventist people in Rochester that Satan's anger had been aroused against them as they had prayed for her husband. She told them that "Satan was determined to make a powerful attack upon them." A short three months later the vision was dramatically fulfilled when Jonathan Orton was murdered. The mystery was never solved.

After her husband's death, Caroline Orton went into a deep depression from which she never really recovered. She died in 1873. J. N. Andrews wrote in the *Review:*

"In 1866 a terrible blow fell upon her in the assassination of her husband. It seemed to her more than she could bear. Unbelief and unreconciliation added to the great bitterness of her cup a still more terrible bitter. Words cannot express the anguish which she has suffered. For several years, however, light has gradually broken into her mind. In her last sickness, which was attended with great pain, her mind was in a state of complete submission to God. . . . We cannot doubt that she sleeps in Jesus."

For more on the Jonathan Orton story, see Ron Graybill, "The Murder of Jonathan Orton," *Insight,* December 5, 1978.

John Loughborough Meets James and Ellen White

John Loughborough met James and Ellen White in late September 1852, just after they returned from extended travels in the eastern part of the country. John was attending the Sabbath service, and it was at that time that he publicly proclaimed his belief in the seventh-day Sabbath.

That same day the Whites invited John to join in the prayer and anointing service for Oswald Stowell, their pressman, who was very sick with pleurisy. The doctor said he could do nothing for the sick man; he faced certain death. As they knelt beside his bed that Sabbath day, Elder White anointed him with oil "in the name of the Lord." They felt the Spirit of God very near to them, and Oswald Stowell was healed instantly. Loughborough reported:

"When we arose from prayer he was sitting up in bed, striking his sides, which before had been so painful, and saying, 'I am fully healed. I shall be able to work the hand press tomorrow.'" Two days later he was again working the hand press.

While they were praying, Ellen White was given a vision. Afterward she told of some of the things that had been revealed to her. For one thing, she had been given information especially for John Loughborough, and we can be certain that he listened carefully. He wrote:

"She spoke to me about the working of my mind before accepting the Sabbath truth. She even knew the thoughts that I had never expressed to anyone. She told of the way I had been treated by my former associates and the less-than-kind way they had spoken to me."

As he heard her tell of these things, he declared to himself, "Surely there is a power more than human connected with this vision."

The Window-Sash Lock Business

After John Loughborough accepted the Sabbath, the sales for his window-sash locks began to drop. In spite of his prayer that the Lord would keep his business going well, he had the distinct impression that the Lord wanted him to devote *all* his time to teaching the Bible truths he had learned. It seemed that God was calling him. But he kept telling himself that he would work hard so he could give financial support to some other minister who could do the work of God better than he could.

Yet the harder he worked, the fewer sales he had. Builders would tell him they planned to use the Arnold window-sash locks, but it would be some time before they were ready to place the order. In the meantime, his savings were used up, and there came a time that he had only one silver three-cent coin in his pocket.

That next Sabbath John came home after the meeting and went upstairs alone to pray. His prayer was "Lord, if You will open the way, I'll go and preach."

As he prayed, his faith grew a little stronger, and he was willing to say, "I'll obey, Lord, and You'll open the way."

Immediately he was filled with relief and thanks to God. His message to himself was "The Lord has told me to go, and the Lord will provide."

Two or three days later his wife was getting ready to go into town. She told him that she needed to buy matches and thread and that she needed money from him to buy them. Putting his hand in his pocket, he brought out the tiny silver coin.

"Mary, here's a three-cent piece," he said, holding it out to her. "It's all the money we have left in the world. Get only one cent's worth of matches, and spend only one other cent. Bring one cent back to me so that we won't be entirely destitute. I've tried to make this business succeed, but I simply can't do it."

Such unexpected words were more than she could handle, and Mary burst into tears. John confessed to her the turmoil that had filled his heart and how he'd finally given it to God.

"Mary, my dear, I feel sure that the reason this lock business isn't succeeding is that I haven't given myself wholly to preaching the truth. When I was praying alone in our room on Sabbath, as soon as I committed myself to obey the call of the Lord He gave me the assurance that He would open the way. I don't know how He'll do it, but I do know that He will."

Mary did a little praying of her own, then put on her coat and went to town. John sat down at the table and continued his Bible study.

About a half hour later there came a knock at the door. John invited the stranger to come in, and the man came directly to the purpose of his visit.

"I'm Mr. Green, from Middleport. I'm moving out to Ohio for my health. I want to have some kind of little business to fill my time and meet my expenses. Thomas Garbut told me that you sell Arnold's patent sash locks. I'd like to buy $80 worth of locks, and I'll ask you to select an assortment of what I might need. I'll pick up the locks tomorrow and pay you then."

Loughborough could only gaze at the man in awe. Then, collecting his wits, he made the deal with Mr. Green, who soon went on his way. The commission on that sale was more than $26, a lot of money at that time. Now Mary could buy all the matches she needed! When she came home, she found him singing.

"Mary," he announced, "while you were gone to town, the Lord opened the way for me to go out and preach."

That $26 supplied their current needs, and John felt comfortable in devoting all his time to whatever God called him to do.

Loughborough's Initiation Into the Traveling Ministry

The very next Sabbath the Lord impressed Hiram Edson, a farmer-preacher in Port Gibson, New York, that he was needed in Rochester immediately. The impression was so strong that he could do nothing but go at once. That very night he took the train for Rochester, getting there about 9:00 p.m.

Taking a hack (a horse-drawn taxi) to 124 Mount Hope Avenue, he knocked on the door. When James White opened it, Edson asked, "What do you want of me? The Lord told me to come immediately."

James White didn't hesitate. "We want you to take old Charlie horse and the carriage," he said, "and take Brother Loughborough on your six-week circuit of New York and Pennsylvania. We want you to get him started in preaching the third angel's message."

Talk about opening the way! Edson and Loughborough spent their first Sabbath on the circuit in Orangeport. A heavy snowstorm made it impossible for them to travel farther by carriage, and it was exchanged for a four-runner box sled, called a "pung." On Christmas Eve 1852 they arrived in Buffalo in a terrible snowstorm. Loughborough had no overcoat. In fact, he had never owned one. Hiram Edson stopped at a store and bought the much-needed coat, and they drove on to Fredonia, where they held meetings for a few days.

At the little town of State Line, New York, Lewis Hacket had made arrangements for Loughborough to speak on Sunday afternoon and evening in a schoolhouse. The morning meeting was to be taken by another minister. Edson and Loughborough decided to attend this meeting to see what the minister had to say. It also would give them opportunity to further advertise their own meetings.

However, when the other minister failed to appear, Loughborough was asked to speak Sunday morning, too. There was a great interest among the congregation, and both the afternoon and evening meetings were packed to overflowing.

The men received a warm welcome all along their route. Many people accepted their message of the Sabbath and the soon coming of Christ, and committed their lives to God.

Homeward at Last

The weather began to moderate, and the snow was melting fast. It was time for the two traveling preachers to turn their horse and sled toward Rochester. They stopped over Sabbath at the home of a family of believers. The man seemed eager to preach the Advent message, but they weren't able to give him much encouragement, for he seemed to be too lazy to be successful in preaching. His wife was out cutting wood to cook his supper while he sat in the parlor with his feet propped up, singing about the easy life he expected to have in heaven. He seemed to take a great deal of pleasure in one particular verse: "We'll have nothing at all to do but march around Jerusalem, when we arrive at home." He seemed to absorb the spirit of this verse by having nothing much to do with labor and toil on earth!

Hiram Edson and John Loughborough had been on the road for about six weeks and had visited more than a dozen companies of Sabbathkeepers, as well as many scattered believers. It was J. N. Loughborough's first preaching tour for the yet-future Seventh-day Adventist Church.

The journey was coming to an end, and by the time the duo reached Attica, New York, the snow had all melted from the road, and they had to walk the last miles to relieve at least some of old Charlie's burden in pulling the heavy sled over bare ground. When they arrived back in Rochester, Loughborough then rode Charlie bareback the 50 miles to Orangeport to retrieve the carriage they had left there in December.

Old Charlie Horse

Elder and Mrs. White's horse Charlie was popular and well known to Sabbathkeepers in the Eastern states. In 1850 the church members in Sutton, Vermont, raised $175 to buy a horse and carriage as a gift of love and support for the Whites. Stagecoach journeys were hard and rough and quickly sapped the energy and strength of travelers. It would be much better for the Whites to have a carriage and horse of their own.

The Whites were given a choice of at least three horses. The first was a high-spirited, nervous sorrel, and Mrs. White's angel guide said, "No. That's not the one."

The next was a large gray horse, to which the angel said, "Not that one."

Then came a beautiful chestnut, to which the angel said, "That's the one for you." His name was Charlie and, in spite of his slight swayback, he served them well and faithfully for many years. He took them not only through the New England states, but to Canada and on toward the West.

Charlie was particularly fond of apples. As they drove through Maine and New Hampshire where orchards lined the country roads, Charlie delighted in selecting a good apple that had fallen into the road. He'd pick it up with his strong teeth, then toss his head into the air and dash down the road at top speed. Yes, old Charlie horse was well known and dearly beloved by the Advent believers.

The Ministers Lost Their Way

John Loughborough and M. E. Cornell were on a preaching tour together in 1853, sometimes holding meetings for two or three days in the same place. Once, as they were getting ready to move on to their next appointment, a man came with an urgent request:

"My boy is sick with a bad fever," he told them. "Will you come and pray for him? He's just 10 years old, and he says that if you'll come and pray for him, Jesus will make him well."

It was late in the day, and going so far out of their way would make it impossible to reach their destination before dark. Regretfully, they had to leave without seeing the boy. After driving along in their buggy for about an hour they came to a gate across the road. They opened it and soon found themselves facing a small house.

The man who had asked them to come and pray for his son came rushing out of the house. "Oh, we're so happy you decided to come. Timmy's been asking for you."

Loughborough and Cornell had been so interested in discussing the Lord's work that they hadn't noticed when the horse made an unscheduled turn and took them directly to the house where the sick boy lay.

They prayed for the youngster, and the Lord healed him immediately. The fever left him, and he got out of bed and felt strong and healthy again. Not only was the boy healed, but the ministers had no problem in reaching their next meeting place before it got too dark to see the way.

Ordained

The first evangelistic tent meeting was held in Battle Creek, Michigan, in 1854, with an estimated 1,000 people in attendance. After the meetings some of the workers met to pray for guidance about where and when to hold more such gatherings. When they rose from their knees, James White made an important pronouncement.

"Brethren, I believe that the time has come for Brother John to be ordained to the gospel ministry. If you are of the same mind, we'll have the ordination ceremony now, tonight."

They were of the same mind, and again the group knelt, this time surrounding young John Loughborough, with Elders White and Cornell laying their hands on the young minister's head. They prayed that the Lord would bless his labors and bring many souls to the kingdom through his work.

There were other ministers in the work at that time who had been ordained in other denominations before joining the Advent believers, but J. N. Loughborough became the first man ordained to the ministry of what was to become the Seventh-day Adventist Church.

Disappointment

By the summer of 1856 Loughborough was feeling discouraged. He didn't know how he was going to make ends meet during the coming winter. He seemed to have forgotten the way the Lord had led him in the not-so-distant past. He received a letter from J. N. Andrews, who, along with about 30 others, had moved to Waukon, Iowa, to take up homesteading. Their plan was to farm and spread the third angel's message, doing the work of missionaries even as they were homesteaders. Loughborough and his wife decided to join the group. It was a way to get a home, make a living, and at the same time spread the gospel.

John and Mary packed up their household and moved to Iowa. Arriving in Waukon, they were sorely disappointed to find that it was a small village out in the middle of nowhere, surrounded by an endless prairie, with only a few farmhouses scattered hither and yon. There was little opportunity for preaching, and shortly after they arrived a foot of snow fell. Then there were alternate thaws, freezes, and more snows. Soon the ground was covered with three layers of ice and snow. Getting from one place to another was almost impossible.

When the weather moderated, Loughborough bought a set of carpenter tools and went to work. One day he and Hosea Mead—one of the believers who had come to Waukon from Washington, New Hampshire—were hammering away on a store building when they heard someone calling their names.

"Come on down!" they heard a man call. "Brother and Sister White and Brother Hart are here in a sleigh."

Mead was excited. "That's Elon Everts' voice! I'd know it anywhere." (Everts was a faithful church member from New Haven, Vermont, who had traveled to Waukon with the Whites.)

The two men quickly put down their tools and hurried to the visitors.

As soon as Loughborough stood beside the sleigh, Mrs. White solemnly asked, "What doest thou here, Elijah?"

She asked him the same question three times, with emphasis on a different word each time, for his answers were obviously not satisfactory.

"*What* doest thou here, Elijah?"

Then "What *doest* thou here, Elijah?"

Then "What doest *thou* here, Elijah?"

John Loughborough was embarrassed. He didn't know what to say. He knew, and Ellen White knew, that hammering nails into a storefront was not the work God had called him to do.

On the night before Christmas all the Adventist families in Waukon met in the home of John and Angeline Andrews. The meetings continued to be held every night from then on through December 31. At one of the meetings Ellen White was given a vision showing what had happened to the group during the months they had been there. Among other things, they had failed to spread the good news of Jesus' soon coming, and they seemed to have lost their first love. They were so busy and tired from trying to make a living that they had little time or energy for telling their neighbors of the love of Jesus. In addition, they had soon begun to find fault with each other, criticizing and becoming bitter.

The Loughboroughs were convinced of their mistake, and they both confessed their failures. "I have laid up my hammer and driven my last nail," John promised. He returned to Illinois with James and Ellen White, while Mary stayed in Waukon until he could make living arrangements for them.

Soon afterward J. N. Andrews also left farming and went back to preaching. Others of the Waukon group followed. Andrews and Loughborough had been rescued for the work of God, and they were never again tempted to turn their backs on it.

Our Home on the Hillside

The year 1865 found Elder Loughborough literally worn out by his constant travel, speaking appointments, and eating "no food fit for human consumption," as he put it. During one of his trips he received word of James White's illness, and he went at once to Battle Creek. The doctors there advised both Loughborough and White to take treatment at Our

Home on the Hillside in Dansville, New York. They spent about 12 weeks there, recuperating from illnesses that had been brought on primarily by overwork. A few years later Loughborough took a one-year medical course, and later he wrote a book entitled *Handbook of Health*. It was a small book on simple methods of healthful living—cleanliness, healthful food, fresh air, etc. It was inexpensive enough that everyone could afford it, and was written in language that everyone could understand. He wrote from what he'd learned in the medical course and from his own experience.

The Tie Is Broken

Through the years the Loughboroughs and Whites were close friends, the men often traveling and working together, the women often visiting in each other's homes. In 1859 Ellen White spent about a month traveling in Michigan with John and Mary and their little girl, Teresa, then 10 months old. James was to have joined them at the end of the first week, but his heavy workload kept him in Battle Creek. Travel with a baby was a real hardship in those days. The roads were rough and in some cases nonexistent, and food was sometimes scarce. At one point they had no milk for little Teresa, and she didn't hesitate to let her frustration be known. Everyone was more than happy when they finally arrived back in Battle Creek and were able to settle into a more normal routine.

A few months later, on the second day of 1860, very early in the morning Elder and Mrs. White were called to the Loughborough home. Baby Teresa was gravely ill, and it was obvious that she was dying. It was a sad day, the Whites watching by the child's bedside and trying to comfort her grieving parents as their little girl died. She was buried in Oak Hill Cemetery in Battle Creek.

On September 20, that same year, the Whites' fourth son, John Herbert, was born. He lived less than two months. A year later Ellen wrote to Mary:

"I went up to Oak Hill Cemetery and fixed our babes' graves and also Clara's [Bonfoey]. Fixed ours exactly alike. Put some pansies on the graves, and some myrtle, and at the foot of the stake put a bunch of tall moss. It looked very pretty. We shall go up again soon and see if the flowers are doing well."

John and Mary Loughborough's second daughter was born on June

24, 1867. Tragically, after the birth something went terribly wrong, and the new mother died about an hour later. John named the baby Mary, after her mother. The Loughboroughs had been married for more than 16 years.

Elder Loughborough's brother and his wife came from New York to take care of his son, Delmer, who was almost 3, and their good friends Myron Cornell and his wife took the newborn baby.

---

* Broughton and Boughton have both been used to identify this individual.

Chapter 17

John Norton Loughborough:
Part 2
California Ho!

At the General Conference session in Battle Creek in May 1868, James White plaintively asked, "Has no one any impressions of duty relative to the California field?"

Actually, John Loughborough had been thinking of California for several months. When Elder White asked his question, John stood and said he was willing to go. Daniel T. Bourdeau rose from his seat and said he would go with him. In fact, Bourdeau had been impressed before coming to the conference that there would be major changes in his working assignments. He and his wife had sold all their household belongings before coming to Battle Creek and were prepared to go wherever the Lord sent them.

Loughborough, also, had been given a number of dreams in which he seemed to take a ship from New York, travel to the Isthmus of Panama, and take another ship to California. The Panama Canal had not yet been built, and ocean travel was via the isthmus. He said that he probably took that trip about 20 times that winter—in his dreams..

It seemed a courageous move to make. In 1868 California seemed as far away as the other side of the world. Getting there would not be easy, and no one knew what they might find when they arrived, After much prayer and counseling, John Loughborough and D. T. Bourdeau made the decision to sail for California and an unknown future.

The two men, along with little Delmer Loughborough and Mrs. Bourdeau, left for New York City on June 8. They spent two weeks buying needed supplies for the journey, as well as an evangelistic tent for their new work in California. It was in New York that John Loughborough married Margaret Newman, with Elder Bourdeau performing the ceremony.

A friend from Battle Creek, who had made the journey to California three times, gave them valuable information on securing tickets at a good price. They were able to save more than $200 by following his advice. They left New York on June 24, 1868. As they went on board the boat, Elder Bourdeau's new $5 hat went tumbling into the water. Loughborough said that "he fretted about it every day until we reached Panama." Apparently there was a great deal of "fretting"—to continue through the entire journey to Panama. After all, $5 was a lot of money.

Their ship arrived in Aspinwall on July 3, and they were taken by tugboat to the steamer *The Golden City*, which lay at anchor a mile from shore. It was two days before they set sail for San Francisco, arriving there on July 18, after 24 days of travel from New York. The voyage had been rough, but the missionaries finally arrived safely at their destination. They were soon planning their meetings, which would begin in Petaluma.

Mr. Wolf's Dream

Even before the Loughborough party embarked on the voyage west, a Mr. Hough, out in California, was studying the Bible with a church group, seeking to find the truth in God's Word. One member of the group had received a newspaper from New York that told about two ministers who would hold religious services in a tent near San Francisco. Mr. Hough's group made these two ministers a subject of prayer in their weekly meeting.

On the night after the prayer meeting another member of the group, Mr. Wolf, dreamed that he was in open country on a dark night. In his dream two men, whom he understood to be ministers, were kindling a fire. The fire soon burned brightly, lighting up the countryside. In the dream he then saw several men try to put out the fire by throwing brush on it. That made it burn even brighter.

The two ministers kept lighting other fires, and the other men kept trying to put them out. Soon there were five fires burning. Mr. Wolf recognized those who were trying to put out the fires as ministers from churches in the community. He heard one of them say, "Let them alone; it's no use. The more we try to put out the fires, the brighter they burn."

In his dream Mr. Wolf also heard that the ones lighting the fires were the two evangelists coming from New York with the tent.

Mr. Hough was sent to find the two ministers from New York. As can be imagined, it could have been like looking for a needle in a haystack; but God miraculously led in tracking them down. When he arrived in San Francisco, Mr. Hough went directly to the Pacific Mail wharf and asked whether a tent had come from Panama on their steamer, *The Golden City*. About that time the deliveryman who had just taken the tent to its temporary destination returned to the warehouse. He told Mr. Hough where he could find the ministers and their tent.

As for the two missionaries, they could only thank God for answering their prayers for an entering wedge. Mr. Hough asked Elders Loughborough and Bourdeau to come to Petaluma the next day to meet his group of people. When he met them at the train station, he said they would stay at his house that night, but they would be entertained for lunch at the home of Mr. Wolf. Wolf wanted to see for himself that they were the same men he had seen in his dream. When he saw them coming toward his house, he exclaimed, "Wife, *there they are;* those are the *identical* men I saw in the dream."

The ministers brought their families to Petaluma, and Mr. Hough helped them find housing and a good location for the tent. He then made arrangements for lumber for seats in the tent. By the second Sunday night of the meeting there weren't enough seats for all the people who came. Mr. Rice, who had somewhat reluctantly lent them the lumber, was so pleased with the success of the meetings that he offered them all the boards they needed for as long as they needed them.

The Lord worked many miracles as John Loughborough and D. T. Bourdeau began their work in California. They reported in the *Review and Herald*:

"A friend who has lived in these parts for 13 years told us that he has never seen so great an interest around here in the discussion of Bible subjects. Members of the churches are already alarmed to see their fellow members flocking out to our meetings. They try to keep them away, but these Californians are too independent for the gag law. They just tell them, 'You can say whatever you want, but I'm going to the meetings anyway!'"

Dr. Parrot Is Healed

Elders Loughborough and Bourdeau began a six-week series of tent meetings on April 22, 1869, in Santa Rosa, California. When the time came for the evangelists to present the Bible doctrine of spiritual gifts, the pastor of one of the largest churches in the area told his people that those gifts were no longer given. He said that those spiritual gifts were given only until the Christian church became established. But it wasn't long until a local miracle of healing called his theory into question and brought even larger crowds to the tent meetings.

A few days prior to the beginning of the meetings a Mrs. Skinner became seriously ill and sent for Dr. Parrot, a woman doctor trained in Europe. After about two weeks Mrs. Skinner was so much better that Dr. Parrot felt she could leave her patient and return to her own home in Windsor. Before going home, however, she planned to spend a few days in Santa Rosa so she could attend the meetings. By late afternoon she was ready to leave, and a horse was harnessed and saddled for her. The plan was for Oliver Skinner, son of the woman who had been ill, to accompany Dr. Parrot and bring the horse back home with him.

The horse lent Dr. Parrot was gentle, safe, and accustomed to women riding sidesaddle. However, when she mounted he began to rear violently, throwing her to the ground. An instant later he crashed down on her, the saddle striking across her arms and chest with such force that the horn was bent straight out. The men in the family picked Dr. Parrot up and took her into the house, but they thought she was already dead.

Eventually she regained consciousness, but couldn't speak above a whisper. Someone suggested sending for a doctor, but she told them that a doctor couldn't help her. She asked them to send for the ministers who were holding meetings in the tent. If they would come and pray, the Lord would heal her.

Oliver Skinner volunteered to go for the ministers, and arrived at the tent just as the meeting was about to open. Elders Loughborough and Bourdeau thought it would be unwise to close the meeting and send the large congregation home, so they promised to come to the Skinner home very early the next morning. Jackson Ferguson readily agreed to take them in his wagon as soon as it was light enough to see, so the next day, before dawn, Elder and Mrs. Loughborough were on their way to the injured woman.

Upon their arrival they learned that it had taken four people to care for Dr. Parrot during the night. When she realized the Loughboroughs were there, she whispered, "Anoint me and pray, and the Lord will heal me." They began to pray most earnestly, placing her in the care of the Great Physician, and Mrs. Loughborough anointed her forehead with oil.

Not many minutes later Dr. Parrot began to pray in a strong voice, not just a whisper. She clapped her hands and in a clear voice announced, "I'm healed! I'm healed!" She rose from the bed, dressed herself, and walked into the next room to see Mrs. Skinner, who was much better but still confined to her bed. Then Dr. Parrot went to the kitchen, where she helped prepare the meal.

The Lord had worked wonderfully in meeting this emergency, and later in the day Dr. Parrot traveled to Santa Rosa with the Loughboroughs. She sat in a chair placed in the lumber wagon, and when they arrived at the tent she enjoyed every moment of the preaching service. She was completely healed and suffered no ill effects from her fall. For good measure, Oliver Skinner, who considered himself an infidel, was so impressed with what he had witnessed that he became a solid witness to all those who inquired into the circumstances of Dr. Parrot's injury. The issue of "spiritual gifts" was settled in that community.

Jackson Ferguson, the man who'd driven Elder and Mrs. Loughborough to the Skinner home in his lumber wagon, had an invalid sister-in-law who was unable to attend the meetings. She asked for Elders Loughborough and Bourdeau to come to her home and teach her some of the things they were preaching at the tent. They were happy to do this and went there about once a week for several weeks. When the time came for her husband's father to be baptized, she told Elder Loughborough that she wanted to be baptized also.

Mrs. Ferguson was dressed and placed in a chair in a wagon that was driven into the river. The two ministers carried her, chair and all, out into deeper water, where she was baptized. As she and her chair were lifted from below the surface of the water, she gave a great, happy shout. Then she rose from the chair, stood for a moment, then walked through the water to the wagon without assistance. Back at her house she changed her wet clothing for dry, and declared herself healed of her illnesses. She then prepared a lunch for her guests. The next Sabbath the congregation at the tent meeting was astonished to see Mrs. Ferguson arrive in a lumber wagon, sit on hardboard seats all through the services, and then return for the evening meeting—all with no ill effect.

By 1871 five churches had been established in Sonoma County, one of them in Santa Rosa, where the first Seventh-day Adventist church west of the Rockies was built in 1869. J. N. Loughborough was one of the first presidents of the California Conference, serving during the 1870s and again in the late 1880s.

The Whites Arrive in California

James and Ellen White arrived in California for the first time in late 1872. They were happy to again be associated in the gospel work with their old friend John Loughborough. They had a good time visiting in the Loughborough home, where they met the second Mrs. Loughborough, Margaret (or Maggie). Ellen White described the home as a large, convenient house of a story and a half, and the Whites were invited to make it their own home for however long they wished. She also thought the two Loughborough children the best, "the most quiet and peaceable," she ever saw. John and Maggie seemed to be very happy, and this made the Whites happy for them.

More Deaths in the Loughborough Family

The two children Mrs. White spoke of were John's children, Delmer and Mary. Their mother, Mary Loughborough, had died an hour after baby Mary was born. Delmer was not quite 3 years old at the time. Their father married Maggie Newman about a year later. At the time of the Whites' visit to their home in the fall of 1872, John and Maggie's baby daughter, Elizabeth Eunice, had recently died at the age of 5 months.

In a sad twist of fate, Maggie Loughborough contracted tuberculosis. Her sister came from the East to take care of her so that John could continue his pioneer work for the Lord. They moved to Woodland, California, and then to St. Helena, where the climate seemed to be better for her. When it came time for the Yountville meetings to begin, men erected a small tent behind the big tent so that Maggie could lie on her bed and hear everything that was said from the rostrum. She was especially interested in reports of the mission work in various places in the West, and her heart beat a little faster as she heard of the progress of the message of truth she loved so dearly.

Throughout her illness Maggie Newman Loughborough remained firm and happy in her belief in the blessed hope that Jesus was coming soon. She died on March 24, 1875, confident in the hope that Jesus would soon come and take her to the glorious home He's preparing for all His children.

Work of the Gospel Moves On

By 1875 there were active, growing churches in both Oakland and San Francisco, and fund-raising plans were under way for building a publishing house in Oakland. A new magazine, *Signs of the Times,* would be published there. Tent meetings and camp meetings flourished not only in California but in Oregon, Nevada, and other territories.

As early as 1874 James White had spoken with Loughborough about the possibility of his going to England to begin a work for the Lord in that country. At the time John couldn't see any wisdom in such a plan, but did commit to seeking the Lord's guidance and will in the matter. They prayed about the situation both separately and together. And on June 6 the two men went into the California mountains, where they prayed for direction concerning the dilemma before them: White needed to know whether he should go east to raise funds for the new publishing work; Loughborough needed to know God's will for him at the present time.

When they arose from their knees, they both were clear as to where their duties lay: James White was to go east and seek the funds to begin publishing *Signs of the Times.* The Loughboroughs were to sell their home in Santa Rosa (they no longer lived there because of Maggie's illness), but not buy anywhere else. He was not to settle in one place but remain free to go where the Lord directed.

Again James asked him if he would go to England, but John replied that he had not received light indicating that his place was there. However, he immediately put his home in the hands of a real estate agent. The man told him that there wasn't much demand for his type of property, but he would see what he could do. Within two weeks the property sold for the asking price. Early the next year Maggie Loughborough died of consumption, and John intensified his traveling itinerary. In addition to his other duties he was asked to serve as president of the new Pacific Press Publishing Association.

Married Again

It may have been during the fourth camp meeting held in California, in September 1875, that John Loughborough married Anna M. Driscol, secretary and treasurer of the Pacific Press, with James White performing the ceremony. The Whites had moved to Oakland earlier in the year and were present at this camp meeting. At any rate, John and Anna were married in 1875.

For John, the next three years were filled with much travel on the West Coast, holding evangelistic tent meetings and camp meetings, as well as carrying out administrative duties.

In the early morning of July 17, 1878, a weary Loughborough boarded the train for Reno, Nevada, where he was to hold an evangelistic tent meeting. He soon fell asleep, still praying for light with regard to going to England. About an hour later he was wakened by what seemed to be a hand shaking him on the shoulder. Thinking it was the conductor, he reached for his ticket, but no one was near him. Although he heard no audible voice, it was as if someone had spoken clearly: "Put up your household goods for sale, and make your arrangements to go to the General Conference [session], and to England, if so decided by the General Conference." This was contrary to his own thinking, but he was willing to leave the matter with God.

He found pen and paper in his bag and immediately wrote to Elder White in Battle Creek, telling his experience. Then he wrote to his wife, Anna, telling her of his experience and asking her to let it be known that their things were for sale. They would then wait and see what happened. If the Lord saw fit to open the way to sell, then he would know it was their duty to go to the General Conference session in Battle Creek.

John fulfilled his duties in Reno, then returned to Oakland to prepare for camp meetings planned in northern and southern California.

As soon as Mrs. Loughborough received his letter, she spread the word among their friends that all their possessions were for sale, right down to table linens and canned fruit. In a few days a man who was planning to be married came and wanted to buy everything they had. He gladly paid the asking price.

Within 10 days of the time John Loughborough had departed for Reno, all their household goods except their clothing and books were sold, and Mrs. Loughborough was staying at the home of J. I. Tay. Both John and Anna felt this was definitely the Lord's leading, and they felt clear to attend the General Conference session, taking the train from Oakland on September 19, 1878. Although the trip took 12 days, it was much shorter than John's monthlong journey from New York to San Francisco 10 years earlier.

Labors in England

That year the General Conference session did vote to begin evangelistic work in England, where William Ings, a literature evangelist, had prepared the way for a larger, more in-depth work. Elder and Mrs. Loughborough were asked to take up that work, and they made preparations to sail from Boston on the steamship *Homer,* of the Warren Line. However, when they arrived on the dock, the agent, Mr. O'Hara, met them with the news that the captain was refusing to take any passengers on board. However, the company would transfer them, free of charge, to the *Nevada,* of the Williams and Guion Line. It would sail from New York the next day.

This was fine with the Loughboroughs, and the next day found them only about 40 yards from the pier from which John had sailed in 1868, en route to San Francisco. After a rough 12-day crossing they arrived safely in Southampton on December 30.

The *Homer,* on which they had been scheduled to sail, was lost at sea and never heard of again. It was speculated that it had been sunk during a storm. It now lay at the bottom of the ocean.

John and Anna Loughborough spent five years in England, establishing a church in Southampton. It was during this time that Maude Sisley, the first single woman missionary called to serve overseas, came from Switzerland to assist Elder Loughborough in his work.

The first General Conference session after the death of James White was held in December 1881. The request came for Loughborough to attend and take a team of workers back with him to England, where he would train them for evangelistic work and send them back for work in America. Those who returned to England with him included Elder and Mrs. A. A. John, George Drew, Jennie Thayer, and Loughborough's own son and daughter, all of whom took part in evangelistic work there.

Returning to America in 1883, Elder Loughborough traveled as a General Conference representative throughout the North Pacific area.

During the next 12 years he held various posts in several conferences. He was president in five conferences and served two terms as the California Conference president. His last presidency was in Illinois, 1891-1895.

Writing and Publishing

Throughout most of his life John Loughborough kept a daily journal, and many incidents of early Adventist history have been preserved through his writings. He wrote dozens of articles for denominational papers and at one time edited the *Pacific Health Journal*. He wrote the first book on denominational history, published in 1892 and titled *The Rise and Progress of Seventh-day Adventists*. It was revised in 1905 as *The Great Second Advent Movement*. Among other books bearing his name is *The Church, Its Organization, Order, and Discipline,* published in 1907. This book was a forerunner of the church manual.

A Visit to Scandinavia

Loughborough's visit to Scandinavia in 1896 got off to a rather unsettling beginning. His boat landed at Southampton, England. From there he traveled by train to London, forgetting that England didn't have the same system of handling luggage as America. When he reached London, he went directly to his appointment, leaving his trunk in the baggage car. He planned to take care of the trunk when he came back to arrange his passage to Sweden. But, unknown to him, his trunk had been set out on the platform in the huge Waterloo station. He didn't have any kind of paperwork to show for it, and the baggagemasters couldn't find even a trace of it. The only marking on the trunk that he could recall was simply "Topeka, Kansas."

He spent two or three anxious days searching for his trunk. He was especially concerned because in the trunk was an irreplaceable manuscript. It was the only copy he had, and there was no way he could re-create it.

Completely exhausted from his luggage search one evening, he returned to the home of Elder and Mrs. W. A. Spicer, with whom he was staying, and lay down on the couch and fell asleep. When he awoke about a half hour later, he was cheerful and happy. He told Mrs. Spicer that he'd had a dream and that everything would be all right. He would find his trunk in Sweden. All his anxiety was gone, for God had given him assurance that all would be well. Just as he expected, when he landed in Sweden, there in a shed on the dock was his trunk.

Anna

John and Anna moved in the early 1900s to Mountain View, California, where they built a small home and planted trees and flowers. John was in his early 70s, and they expected to live happily until the Lord came. But the bubble of their dream burst when Anna died on May 31, 1907. They had been married for almost 32 years, and now John was alone again. But his faith and hope in the resurrection were intact, and he still had things to do for his Lord.

Around the World

When Elder Loughborough was 76 years old, the General Conference Committee asked him to make a 16-month trip around the world. He visited many mission stations and churches, as well as hospitals and publishing houses. During this trip he traveled 30,000 miles by sea and 17,500 miles on land, preaching 352 times. Speaking of the trip later, he said he wasn't sick even a day and he didn't miss a meal. In fact, he said he almost felt young again.

Ellen White's Funeral at Elmshaven

John Loughborough had long been Ellen White's close friend and associate. After her death in 1915, the first of three funerals was held on the lawn of her Elmshaven home. Elder Loughborough was invited to give her life sketch.

About 400 people gathered on the lawn to say their goodbyes to the "little white-haired lady who always spoke so lovingly of Jesus." It was a simple service, at which the participating ministers were those who had been associated with Mrs. White for many years. In his life sketch Loughborough mentioned that God had given her a vision within a few hours of his first meeting her in 1852; then he recounted other experiences he had witnessed through the years.

He Walked Humbly With His God

Alonzo Baker related an experience he and a friend had with Elder

Loughborough when they were teenagers. It was 1909, and Elder Loughborough was holding a series of evening meetings in the Healdsburg, California, church. It was winter, and the church was heated by large woodburning stoves, one in the rear of the sanctuary and the other at the front. Alonzo Baker, age 15, and Bennie Grant, age 13, were the janitors, and they were sitting in the last row of the sanctuary. They were there to be sure the fires in the stoves were kept burning.

As boys do, they were whispering and laughing, paying no attention to the speaker. Suddenly they became aware that Elder Loughborough had stopped speaking and was staring straight at them. After what seemed quite a long pause, he spoke directly to them. "I wish that Lonnie Baker and Bennie Grant back there by the stove would cease their whispering," he said, "for I am saying some things I think they need in order to be better Christian boys."

Of course, everyone turned to see what was happening. Among them were Bennie's mother and two aunts, and Alonzo's sister, Alma Baker McKibbin. Needless to say, both boys received further admonition on their way home.

Fourteen years later, in 1923, Alonzo received a letter from Elder Loughborough, written from St. Helena Sanitarium, where he now made his home. By that time Alonzo was an associate editor of *Signs of the Times* in Mountain View, California. Bennie Grant was a medical doctor, a graduate of what is now Loma Linda University School of Medicine. In his handwritten letter Elder Loughborough extended his apologies:

"Dear Elder Alzono Baker: Thirteen years ago when I was holding a series of meetings in the Healdsburg church, I was unnecessarily harsh and severe with you and Bennie Grant. I humiliated you two boys in front of all that large congregation, a thing I should not have done.

"I am now reviewing my entire life to prepare to meet the Lord someday, and the episode in Healdsburg in 1909 came vividly into my mind. I ask you and Bennie Grant to forgive me. I have already asked God's forgiveness for this grievous thing I did. Inasmuch as I do not have Bennie Grant's address, will you please send this letter on to him?

"I hope my rebuke did not discourage you two boys in your Christian experience, for I want to meet you both in the kingdom of heaven.

"In sincere penitence, your brother, J. N. Loughborough."

Elder Baker felt that he and Bennie had deserved the rebuke and that the older man had not been unnecessarily harsh and severe with them. It had been good for them, he said. But that experience in 1909, along with his letter of 1923, seemed to them proof positive of Elder Loughborough's character and humility.

The Last of the Original Pioneers

As mentioned above, the St. Helena Sanitarium was home to John Loughborough during his later life. He enjoyed the fresh air of the solarium and spent some time there each day. One afternoon while he was reading the *Review* a young nurse came by and remarked to him that she had heard that he had read every *Review* that had been printed. With a twinkle in his eyes the old gentleman replied that it wasn't true. The nurse lifted her eyebrows in surprise, and after a short pause he replied, "After I have finished reading this one, then I will have read them all."

J. N. Loughborough died on April 7, 1924—the last of the original pioneers of the Advent movement. They all wait in the grave for Jesus to come and raise them to life everlasting, resting under the benediction "Blessed are the dead, which die in the Lord . . . that they may rest from their labors, and their works do follow them."

John Norton Loughborough's works surely do follow him, and most assuredly he "will see his Lord a-coming."

Bibliography

Ellen G. White Estate document files, letter and manuscript files, question and answer files.

Ford, Mark. *The Church at Washington, New Hampshire.* Hagerstown, Md.: Review and Herald Pub. Assn., 2002.

Gordon, Paul A., and James R. Nix. *Laughter and Tears of the Pioneers.* Brushton, N.Y.: Teach Services, 1987.

Hook, Milton. *Flames Over Battle Creek.* Washington, D.C.: Review and Herald Pub. Assn., 1977.

Insight, Dec. 5, 1978.

Knight, Anna. *Mississippi Girl.* Nashville: Southern Pub. Assn., 1952.

Lantry, Eileen. *Miss Marian's Gold.* Mountain View, Calif.: Pacific Press Pub. Assn., 1981.

McKibbin, Alma E. *Step by Step.* Washington, D.C.: Review and Herald Pub. Assn., 1964.

Ministry, December 1975.

Nix, James R. *Early Advent Singing.* Hagerstown, Md.: Review and Herald Pub. Assn., 1994.

Pacific Union Recorder, Apr. 3, 1967; Aug. 26, 1968; Dec. 9, 1968.

Review and Herald, Nov. 25, 1851; Mar. 19, 1857; Sept. 15, 1868; May 13, 1873; Mar. 25, 1884; Feb. 3, 1885; May 18, 1916; Mar. 31, 1955.

Robinson, Ella M. *Lighter of Gospel Fires.* Mountain View, Calif.: Pacific Press Pub. Assn., 1954.

———. *S. N. Haskell: Man of Action.* Washington, D.C.: Review and Herald Pub. Assn., 1967.

Robinson, Virgil. *James White.* Washington, D.C.: Review and Herald Pub. Assn., 1976.

Seventh-day Adventist Encyclopedia. Hagerstown, Md.: Review and Herald Pub. Assn., 1996.

Spalding, Arthur W. *Footprints of the Pioneers*. Washington, D.C.: Review and Herald Pub. Assn., 1947.

———. *Pioneer Stories of the Second Advent Message*. Nashville: Southern Pub. Assn., 1922, 1942.

———. *Pioneer Stories Retold*. Washington, D.C.: Review and Herald Pub. Assn., 1956.

Spicer, William A. *Pioneer Days of the Advent Movement*. Washington, D.C.: Review and Herald Pub. Assn., 1941.

———. *The Spirit of Prophecy in the Advent Movement*. Washington, D.C.: Review and Herald Pub. Assn., 1927.

Wehtje, Myron F. *And There Was Light*. South Lancaster, Mass.: Atlantic Press, 1982.

Wheeler, Gerald. *James White*. Hagerstown, Md.: Review and Herald Pub. Assn., 2003.

White, Arthur L. *Ellen G. White*. Washington, D.C.: Review and Herald Pub. Assn., 1981-1986. Vols. 1-6.

White, Ellen G. *Colporteur Ministry*. Mountain View, Calif.: Pacific Press Pub. Assn., 1953.

———. *Early Writings*. Mountain View, Calif.: Pacific Press Pub. Assn., 1882.

———. *Life Sketches*. Mountain View, Calif.: Pacific Press Pub. Assn., 1915.

———. *Selected Messages*. Washington, D.C.: Review and Herald Pub. Assn., 1958, 1980. Books 1, 3.

William C. White correspondence files.

Ellen White Series
by George R. Knight

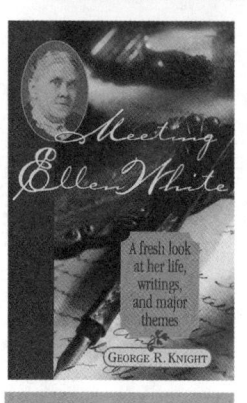

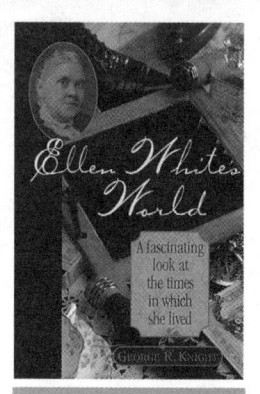

Meeting Ellen White

Introduces readers to the fascinating life and role of Ellen White. The author presents a biographical overview of her life and explores the major themes and categories of her works. Especially helpful for new Adventists. Paperback. 0-8280-1089-7.

Reading Ellen White

A look at issues that have long been at the heart of Adventist understandings and misunderstandings of their prophet: the need for interpretive principles, her relation to the Bible, the purpose of her writings, and principles for interpreting and applying them. Paperback. 0-8280-1263-6.

Ellen White's World

This fascinating look at the world in which Ellen White lived provides a deeper appreciation and understanding of her writings. Includes many photographs and drawings illustrating life in the late 1800s and early 1900s. Paperback. 0-8280-1356-X.

Walking With Ellen White

Here is an intimate glimpse into Ellen White's personal life—her joys and struggles as a wife, mother, friend, and Christian. Paperback. 0-8280-1429-9.

REVIEW AND HERALD® PUBLISHING ASSOCIATION

3 Ways to Shop
- Visit your local Adventist Book Center®
- Call 1-800-765-6955
- Order online at AdventistBookCenter.com